AN AMERICAN HOBO IN EUROPE

AN AMERICAN HOBO IN EUROPE

WINDY BILL (BEN GOODKIND)

ISBN: 978-93-89679-67-0

Published: -

LECTOR HOUSE LLP
E-MAIL: lectorpublishing@gmail.com

AN AMERICAN HOBO IN EUROPE

A TRUE NARRATIVE OF THE ADVENTURES OF A POOR AMERICAN AT HOME AND IN THE OLD COUNTRY

BY

WINDY BILL

CONTENTS

CHAPTER I.

BILLY AND ME.

Stranger, will you please permit me to give you an introduction to a particular friend of mine, little Billy. Little Billy and I had long been friends and had become so intimate that we were more like brothers than friends. Some brothers indeed do not stick to each other as closely as Billy and I did for we never quarreled and the worst that ever happened between us was a little growl which we soon got over.

Billy and I had been on the bum together a long while and had prospected for gold and other things in Utah, Nevada and California. The adventures we had if I were to relate them would fill several such volumes as this. And many of them were worth relating, too, but I will merely give a general outline of our experiences, for his experiences were mostly mine.

While hiking it along the railroad one day between Ogden and Salt Lake City which is a distance of about thirty-seven miles, we ran across a couple of pretty Mormon girls about half a mile from town and they made goo-goo eyes at us. Billy, who is rather reserved with strangers, was for moving on, but I, who am a friendly and sociable cuss, was in for having a little time with them.

"What's the harm, Billy?" said I to my chum; "let's see what kind of stuff the girls are made of."

"Oh, what's the use, Windy," responded Billy; "we might get into trouble."

"Trouble be blowed," said I; "they ain't agoing to make any trouble so why should *we*. Let's see what their game is anyway."

We approached the ladies, tipped our hats, and passed the compliments of the day. They responded pleasantly enough, entered into a conversation with us and soon we all strolled further on from the town and sat down on a viaduct spanning a rushing irrigation ditch. Billy was as chipper as anyone when once he got started and held his end down in the conversation first class. The girls were merry and talkative and seemed to like to talk to the fellers. They told us all about the Mormons, how they live, act, and what they do, and Billy wanted to know how Mormons got married.

"Why don't you get married and find out?" asked one of the girls.

"I ain't no Mormon," spoke up Billy.

"You can be if you want to," says the girl, "religion is free."

"All right," says Billy, "I'll think it over."

The girls were giving us a game I thought, but we could stand it if they could. We chinned away there for hours until it began to grow late, when the girls concluded they would have to go. We were sorry to part from such elegant company but it was a case of have to.

After they had gone we wondered what their little game was, whether it was merely a case of flirtation or whether they were looking for converts to their religion. Billy put the question to me and I told him he could search me; I didn't know. Anyway, neither of us wanted to get married just then, so after the girls left us we troubled our heads no more about them.

We stopped in Ogden, Utah, a few days, and then beat our way to Virginia City, Nevada, where we did some laboring work at the old Bonanza mines. Neither of us were miners, although we had prospected some without results. We found the miners to be a good-hearted set of fellows and liked to be among them. Grub and booze could be had for the asking in Virginia City when we were broke, but handouts were more plentiful than work. Not many strangers wander to Virginia City these days, for the town is off the main line and no bums visit it. It is on the decay order. Its streets are in ruins, ditto the sidewalks and houses, and over the whole place there is a musty odor. It is away high up in the air about eight thousand feet above sea level and the wealth that once was brought up from several thousand feet below the surface amounted to billions, not millions of dollars. Today the big mill houses still stand in their usual place in good order but little mining is done there.

Some of the big plants, such as the Ophir, Savage, Norcross and Hale, Consolidated Virginia and Best & Belcher are still there, but where there were a thousand miners working before there are not ten working today. The place is strictly on the bum, just like me and my little pardner. Once there were forty or fifty thousand people in Virginia City, but today there are not five thousand, or anyways near that number and the ruins and scenes of desolation make a fellow feel sad. The old International Hotel where the nobs used to stop and spent a fortune every day, is now run by a Chinaman at a cheap rate. There is plenty of fine scenery around Virginia City, however, and plenty of Piute Indians, but the Piutes don't enhance the scenery any. They are a dirty crowd and sit around on decaying lumber piles and hillsides within the town, playing cards and other gambling games. The miners are mostly Cornishmen, Englishmen from Cornwall, England, and as Billy is English he took to them very readily.

Carson was our next stopping place and we found it to be a nice little town. It isn't far from Virginia City and is the capital of Nevada. It contains a few thousand people, lots of tall poplar trees which stand along the streets, sage-brush and alkali covered hills and plains, a large stone railroad roundhouse, the State Capitol building (which is enclosed in a park several acres in extent), a U. S. mint and that's about all. No work to speak of is going on around there and as Billy and me could not get anything to do we lived on hand-outs mostly. One evening we saw a hen wandering about rather aimlessly, so to put her out of misery we caught her, wrung her neck and took her out of town where we roasted her over a slow fire. We rubbed her while she was cooking with a little sage to make us think of

Christmas and devoured her by starlight. Bill said she reminded him of home and felt kind of blue for a few moments. But he munched away and soon cheered up.

It may be the proper thing here to give a short description of Billy.

Billy was a little fellow, about five foot two, and was a Britisher, a native of the city of York, in Yorkshire, after which New York is named. He was what you might call a strawberry blonde, for he had light hair and a moustache that was halfway between golden and red. It wasn't one of your straggly kind of moustaches with big hairs sticking out all over it, but small, neat and compact with just the cutest little turned up spit-curls at each end of it you ever saw. Maybe Billy wasn't proud of that moustache! He was dead stuck on it and was nearly always fussing with it and fondling it. Quite often he trimmed it with the aid of a little looking glass which he carried in his kit. Whenever the kit was unrolled Billy got the glass and admired himself with it. And yet I can't say the little cuss was vain, for whenever he met females he seemed indifferent to their charms and looked another way. His eyes were blue and his hands and feet small. Taken all together he wasn't a bad looking chap. Billy had some folks in the old country, a mother and two sisters but no father or brothers, and they lived in old York. Billy was born and raised in York and at a very early age was apprenticed to a harness-maker. His folks probably thought that the sooner he got out and rustled the better for himself and all concerned. Apprentices don't get much in old England, Billy told me, and have to serve long years at their trade before they can become a journeyman. Billy worked seven or eight years for his clothes and board and an occasional ha-'penny with which he bought a meat pie or lollipops.

One day the idea struck him that he wasn't getting rich very fast. He had been working a long time and hadn't a bean to show for it, so he began to grow dissatisfied. He had heard some tales of how easy it is to get rich in America and he thought that it might be a good thing if he went there. His mother and sisters didn't agree with his notions but Billy didn't seem to care for that. He just laid low for awhile and said nothing. But the more he thought things over the more dissatisfied he became and the more determined to flit. He slept in the back room of his boss's shop and had to arise early every morning to take down the shutters, sweep out, dust off, and get things in shape generally for business.

One day the boss came down and found the shutters still up, the place unswept and no Billy. The boss probably wondered where little Billy was but he had to take it out in wondering, for Billy had flown the coop and was over the hills and far away on his way to London. The boss went to Billy's folks and asked them if they knew where Billy was, but they told him he could search them. They didn't know anything about Billy. The boss probably did some pretty tall cussing just then and made up his mind that something would happen to Billy when he turned up, but he never did turn up and never will until he (Billy) gets rich. Then he'll go back to visit his folks and settle with his master, he told me. Billy says the boss don't owe him any money and he don't owe the boss any, so it's a standoff financially between them; but Billy owes him a few years of service which he says he is willing to put in if the boss can catch him. Billy says he had a hard time of it in London and found it difficult to secure passage to this country. Finally, after many heart-breaking experiences he secured a job as steward on an ocean liner by a fluke, merely because another chap who had previously been engaged failed to show up. Billy was in luck, he thought. He landed in New York with a little tip-money, for the steamship company would pay him no wages unless he made the round trip according to an agreement previously made in London and with this small sum of money he managed to live until he found work. He secured a job as dishwasher in a restaurant and received five dollars a week and his chuck as wages. Out of this big sum he paid room rent and managed to save a little money which he sent home to his mother. Compared with what he had been getting in the old country Billy considered that he was on the road to fortune and he felt elated. He held down his job for some months but got into a difficulty one day with his boss over something or other and got fired. He took his discharge much to heart and concluded to leave New York. He made his way to Philadelphia, about one hundred miles west, and there secured work in a small restaurant as a hashslinger. When he left this place because of a little argument with another waiter, he concluded to go out West where he was told the opportunities were great. I met him in a camp seated at a fire one evening surrounded by a lot of 'bos in Wyoming. He didn't look wealthy just then. We scraped up an acquaintance and I took to the young fellow at the first go-off as I saw he was not a professional vag, and we joined forces and have been together ever since.

Our trip from Carson in Nevada over the mountains into California was a delightful one. From Carson to Reno the scenery is no great shakes (although it was over hill and dale), for the hills looked lone and barren. The crops had just been gathered from these hills and dales. The leaves were turning color on the trees and it was the melancholy season of the year when nature looks blue. Me and Billy weren't melancholy, however, for we were good company to each other and never felt lonely. At Reno early one morning we crept into an unsealed boxcar and rode upward to the high Sierras. The scenery when day broke was so fine that we were enchanted. No barren mountains were here and no sage-brush covered plains, but well-timbered mountains whereon grew trees and bushes of all kinds. To us it seemed like wakening from autumn to spring. Billy and me couldn't understand this. A few miles away were leaves that were turning in their autumn tints whilst here everything was green and fresh like the dawning of life. It astonished us but made us feel good all over. We were both as happy and joyous as if we were millionaires. Here was a beautiful sheet of water with a big paper-mill near it; further along was a little railroad station entirely surrounded by hills. Nothing but lofty mountains towered all around us, with a canyon running through them, along which we rode. Ice-ponds were there with no ice in them just then, for it was the wrong season for ice, but numerous huge ice-houses were there, which showed us what the ponds were for. The iron horse wound around and around these lofty mountains and the keen, pure air made us feel as good as if we had been taking a nip. We sure felt gay and happy as larks. By-and-by we reached a place called Truckee which seemed to be quite a town. We hopped off to reconnoiter for we knew the freight train would be there some little time, and noticed that there was only one street in the town, which contained several stores, a butcher-shop or two, several restaurants, two hotels and about a dozen or more saloons. As we walked along the street we noticed a sign over a stairway leading into a cellar which read, "Benny's Gray Mule." We started to go down the steps but found that "Benny's Gray Mule" was shut up tight. Too bad! A saloon with such a romantic name as that ought to thrive. We went into another saloon and I ordered two beers and threw a dime upon the counter in payment. "Come again," said Mr. Barkeep, giving me an evil glance. I hesitated. "Another dime, pardner, all drinks are ten cents here," says barkeep. "All right," says I, "don't get huffy; I didn't know the price." I laid down another dime and this Mr. Barkeep swept into his till nonchalantly.

The place seemed tough and so did the barkeeper. Toward the rear of the large room was a lunch counter where a square meal could be had for two bits (25 cents), or coffee and hot cakes for fifteen cents; sandwiches for a dime each; a piece of pie and coffee, ten cents. In convenient places were gambling layouts where a fellow could shoot craps, play roulette or stud-horse poker. It was too early in the day for gambling but a few tough-looking nuts were there sitting around and waiting for a chance to try their luck. We saw all we wanted of this place and sloped. Truckee is the last big town in California going eastward, and it is a lumber camp, railroad division and icing station (refrigerator cars are iced there). A pretty rough old place it is. Me and Billy bought a couple of loaves of bread and some cheese and then made tracks for our box-car. We found it all right and climbed aboard. Our train had done a lot of switching at Truckee and a good many cars had been added to the train. Two big engines now were attached to the train instead of one and soon with a "toot toot" we were off. It was uphill all the way and the locomotives seemed to be having a hard time of it for their coughs were loud and deep and the hissing of steam incessant. To Billy and me the work was easy for all we had to do was to listen to the laboring engines and look out at the pretty scenery. The scenery was fine and no mistake, for the higher we went the prettier it got. Mountains we saw everywhere with spruce, fir, pine and cedar trees upon them. The views were ever changing but soon we came to a lot of snow-sheds that partly shut off the views. They must have been a hundred miles in length, for it took us an awful long time to get through them. The sheds were huge affairs of timber built over the track to keep off the snow in winter, and I felt like stopping and counting how many pieces of timber were in each shed. It must have taken a forest to build these sheds.

Along in the afternoon we began to get hungry, so we jumped off at a place called Dutch Flat, to see what we could scare up in the shape of a handout. The outlook didn't seem promising to us for all we could see of Dutch Flat was a lot of Chinese shacks strung along one side of the railroad track.

"Billy, I guess we're up against it here," I remarked; "I don't see any signs of a white man's house around. Where can we get anything to eat?"

"Let's try the Chinks; we've got to have something to eat, you know; we can't starve," ruefully responded Billy.

We were both pretty hungry by this time for the bracing mountain air had given us a hearty appetite.

I stepped up to the first hut we came to, rapped at the door and when a chink opened it told him we were very hungry and would like something to eat.

"No sabee," says the chink, slamming the door.

I tried other huts with the same result. It was "no sabee" with all of them. I told Billy that my errand was a failure and his jaw dropped.

"How much money have you got, Billy?" I asked.

Billy dug down and brought up a lone nickel. I had a dime. I asked Billy to give me his nickel and told him that as we couldn't beg any grub maybe we might be able to buy fifteen cents' worth of something. With the fifteen cents I strode forth to try my luck once more.

I saw a very old Chinaman in front of his hut and asked him if he would sell me fifteen cents worth of grub.

"No gotee anything; only law (raw) meat."

"What kind of meat?"

"Pork chop," answered the old man, briefly.

"All right, here's fifteen cents; give me some meat."

I handed him the money and he went inside and brought out two fair sized chops.

"You sabee cookee?" asked the aged celestial.

"Heap sabee, you bet; me cookee before," remarked I.

"All lightee," said the celestial, giving me a little salt and pepper.

The country around Dutch Flat was hilly so Billy and me hunted up some secluded spot where we could eat our chops in peace and quietness. We built a rousing fire, for wood around there was plentiful, and put the chops upon long sticks which we hung over the fire. The grass around our camp was pretty dry and the first thing we knew the fire began to spread all over the country. When we stamped it out on one side it made good headway on the other side, and do all we could we couldn't stop it. We got scared, dropped our meat and sloped. It wasn't long before the Chinamen saw the fire and then there was a whole lot of loud talk in Chinese. The whole village was out in a jiffy with buckets, pails, empty oil cans and any old thing that would hold water and at it they went, trying to put out the fire. Not a few of the Chinamen procured wet sacks with which they tried to beat out the flames, but it was no go. Me and Billy returned and grabbed a sack each, wet it and aided all we could in putting out the fire, but it had gained too much headway and defied us all. I concluded that it was going to burn down all the Sierra mountains before it got through. There was a laundry in the Chinese village for I noticed a lot of white man's underwear and white shirts hanging on lines to dry, and near by was the washerman's horse tethered to a stake. When the horse saw and smelt the flames he became frantic and was a hard horse to hold. His owner ran up and yelled and shouted at him in Chinese but the horse either did not or would not understand what was said to him for he tried to kick the stuffing out of his boss and everything else that came near him. He kicked down every wash line that he could, one after another, and did his best to break loose from his halter, but it was no go. He wouldn't let his boss get anyway near him for his heels flew in every direction and it made us laugh to hear the Chinamen swear in Chinese. After the brute kicked down every line within reach of his heels he finally broke loose and galloped over the hills at a breakneck pace. For all that Billy and I know to the contrary he is galloping yet. Billy and me concluded that it was about time for us to skip out, too, so we did so. We had done all we could to help put out the fire and lost our grub in the operation, so we felt that we had done our duty. I have often thought of that fire since and wondered what the result was, whether it ended in great damage to the country and the destruction of the Chinese village, or whether the horse had ever showed up again. There is no rainfall in California during the summer months, I am told, and in consequence the grass and much of the vegetation dries up and one has to be very careful where to light a fire. We didn't know that, hence the disaster.

We climbed into our car again, and were ready to move on whenever the train did. We lit our pipes, indulged in a smoke, and laughed over our recent experience. We must have laughed pretty loud, for a head was suddenly thrust into the car doorway and a stern visage confronted us. It was the brakeman's. "What you fellers doin' there?" asked Brakey.

"Only taking a ride," responded Billy.

"Where to?" asked Brakey.

"Down the line a little way."

"What are you riding on?" asked Mr. Brakeman.

"On a freight train," innocently answered Billy.

I guffawed, for I knew Billy had given the wrong answer, but Brakey never cracked a smile.

"Got any money or tickets?" asked he, gravely.

"No," answered Billy.

"Get off then and be quick about it," was the stern command.

Off we hopped and quite crestfallen, too, for our journey for the time being was ended. We wandered back to the railroad station to ascertain when the next train would leave. There would be nothing until early the next morning we learned, so there was nothing for us to do but to unroll our blankets and lay off somewhere near by where we could catch a train as it came by. We were very hungry, but turned in supperless, and chewed tobacco to satisfy the cravings of our stomachs. We soon fell asleep but kept one ear open to catch the sound of any freight train coming our way. Wayfarers are wonderfully acute, even in their sleep, as regards noticing the approach of trains. No matter how sound their sleep may be, they will wake up at the proper time to board a train nine times out of ten, unless they are too badly boozed. During the early hours of the morning a long train full of empty cars came our way and we made it easily. It was mighty chilly at that time of the day, but as we had on heavy overcoats, our bodies did not suffer much. Our feet, however, did. Fellows who beat their way, though, must put up with such little inconveniences without kicking. It belongs to the business. They must bear hunger, cold, thirst, dust, dirt and other trifles of that kind and get used to it. Those who travel in Pullman and tourist cars pay their money and sleep on feathers, but we slept just as well and nearly as warmly, wrapped in our blankets in a box car. During our wanderings we slept on the ground, in old shacks, barns, sidetracked cars or any old place and got along fairly well. We didn't have washbasins to wash in, but we carried soap, brushes and hand-glasses with us, and could make our toilet at any place where there was running water. Water was plentiful in the Sierra mountains.

We pulled out of Dutch Flat when the train got ready and flew down the mountain side at great speed. We could go as lively as the train could in our car, however, and the speed was exhilarating, but the morning breeze was mighty keen and cutting. We would have given a great deal for a cup of hot coffee just then, but of course it wasn't to be had.

When we neared a place called Auburn we saw a grove of trees, the leaves of which were a deep green, and among them hung little balls of golden yellow fruit that looked good to us.

"Hi, Billy," exclaimed I, "look at them yellow balls hanging on the trees, will you? Wonder what they are?"

Billy looked at them fixedly for quite a while and then suddenly made a shrewd guess.

"Them's oranges, Windy, as sure as we're alive."

These were the first oranges Billy or I had ever seen growing on trees and they surely looked good to us. They reminded us of Christmas trees. We would liked to have jumped out to get some oranges for breakfast, but they were so near and yet so far that we desisted. How tantalizing it was to see a tempting breakfast before you and not be able to eat it. But the train didn't stop anywhere for refreshments, so that let us out. When we got down to a place called Roseville, which was a junction, we noticed several orange trees standing near the depot with plenty of oranges hanging amid the leaves, and oh, how we did long to make a rush for them. The train crew was on that side of the train, however, and there were plenty of people near the depot so we dared not make the venture. Oh, if this train would only stop twenty minutes for refreshments maybe we could get a handout, but it didn't stop, so we had to go hungry till we reached Sacramento.

We got to Sacramento, the Capital of California, before noon, and jumped off the train in the railroad yard, keeping an eye on the bulls and fly-cops that buzzed around there. No one got on to us so we walked leisurely along with our blankets slung over our shoulders. The railroad yards were quite extensive and it took us quite a while to traverse them. In them were car shops, foundries and all kinds of buildings and things pertaining to railroads. Sacramento is a railroad division, the first out of Frisco, I believe, and we noticed a good deal doing in the way of railroad manufacturing, but we were too hungry to care for such things just then. We got to the passenger train shed which was a large housed-over building of glass and iron, and outside of it came upon a broad street which led into the town. Alongside of this street I noticed a slough with green scum upon it which didn't look good to me for swimming or any other purpose. On the other side of this pond was a big Chinatown and Billy and me thought we might as well see what it looked like. We entered it and saw a young workingman come out of a ten-cent restaurant. Billy stepped up to him and boned him for the price of a square meal. He listened to Billy's hungry tale of woe and coughed up a dime with which we bought two loaves of bread. We then wandered through the streets looking for a retired spot where we could sit down and eat but the streets in that locality were so filthy and the Mongolians so plentiful that we concluded to keep a moving. We came to J and then to K Street, which were broad business thoroughfares full of stores and then we walked along K Street until we saw a shady green park. To it we wandered and found a comfortable rustic seat under the shade of a spreading oak tree. We threw our blankets behind our seat and sat down and blew off steam. We were tired, hot, dusty and hungry. While eating we looked about us. The park wasn't a large one but it was a trim one. The lawns were shaved down close, the winding walks were well-kept, there were flowers to be seen, palm trees, pampas-plume bushes and, oh ye gods! orange trees with oranges on them.

"Say Billy," remarked I with my mouth full of bread, "get on to the orange trees, will you?"

"Where?" asked Billy, with wide-staring eyes.

"Why, right along the walk up that way," said I, pointing.

"Sure enough," says Billy, "keep an eye on my grub, will you, while I get a hatful," said he excitedly.

"Keep your eyes peeled for cops," admonished I, as Billy rushed off.

Billy made the riffle all right and came back with four or five nice looking oranges, which were all he could carry. He remarked that they would do for the present. After stowing the bread and getting a drink of muddy water from a fountain near by, we tackled the oranges and found them dry and tasteless and bitter as gall.

"Call them things oranges!" sneered Billy, as he threw his portion away with disgust; why they're bitter as gall. I've bought many a better orange than that in the old country for a penny.

"I thought they raised good oranges in California," said I, "but if they're all like these, then I don't want any of them," whereupon I threw mine over my shoulder, too, into the shrubbery behind me. Oh, weren't they bitter; Boo!

"Billy, we've been misinformed," said I, "the oranges in California are N. G."

"Right you are, Windy, but as they didn't cost us anything we oughtn't to kick."

After eating and resting, we took in the town. We found Sacramento to be a sizeable place, containing about fifty thousand people, and the people to us seemed sociable, chatty and friendly. We both liked the place first class, and as we were broke, concluded to try our luck there for awhile. We struck a street cleaning job and held it down for a week. The water used in Sacramento comes from the Sacramento river, we were told, and as it wasn't at all good, we took to beer, as did many others. We were told about a class of people in Sacramento called Native Sons, who monopolized all the good things in the way of jobs. Native Sons are native born Californians who take a great deal of pride in their state and have an organization which they call the Native Sons of the Golden West. The aim of this organization is to beautify California, plant trees, keep up the old missions, preserve the giant redwood trees, forests, and the like. Lots of fellows spoke ill of the Native Sons, but we didn't, for they weren't hurting us any. The native Californians we met in Sacramento to us seemed a genial sort of people who are willing to do strangers or anyone a good turn, if they can. Lots of them were hustlers and full of business and their city surely is a snorter. There are several large parks in Sacramento, fruit and vegetable markets, and any number of swell saloons where a schooner of beer and a free lunch can be had for a nickel. Then there is the Western Hotel, State House and Capitol Hotels, all of which are big ones, and any number of fine stores and lots of broad, well-shaded residence streets, traction cars, electric lights, etc. The city is right up to date.

After we had been there about a week, Billy suddenly got a severe attack of the shakes and seemed in a bad way. His lips turned blue, his eyes burned with fever, his teeth rattled like clappers, and his body shook as if he had the jim-jams. I went to a dispensary and had some dope fixed up for him, but it didn't seem to do him any good. I then bought a quart bottle of whiskey, and poured the whole of it down his throat. He took to it as naturally as a kid does to its mother's milk, but every day the poor little cuss got worse.

"Let's hike out of this place, Billy," said I; "the best cure for the shakes is to go where there isn't any, for as long as we stay here you'll be sick."

Billy, as usual, was willing to do as I said (and I was always willing to do as he said), so we made tracks out of Sacramento in pretty short order.

We crossed the Sacramento river, which is about a half a mile across, on a wooden bridge, and it was all Billy could do to walk across it. He was as weak as a kitten and so groggy on his pins that he could hardly stand up. Some people who saw him probably thought he was boozed, but he wasn't, any more than I was. I took hold of his arm and led him along, but the little cuss sat down on a string piece of the bridge and told me to let him die in peace.

"Die nothing, you silly little Britisher: you ain't any nearer death than I am," said I. "Sit down and rest yourself and then we'll take another little hike. We'll make a train somewhere on the other side of the river, then ho! for 'Frisco, where our troubles will soon be ended. Brace up, old man, and never say die."

I jollied the little cuss along in that way until we got to a little station where we could catch a train and we soon did catch one.

We rode on to Davis, which was a junction, and close to the station I saw a large vineyard. I pointed it out to Billy.

"Stay where you are, Billy, and I'll get you some grapes," said I.

Grapes were ripe just then. I jumped over the fence and secured a big hatful of fine big, flaming tokay grapes. They were delicious and did Billy a world of good.

We were now fairly on our way to 'Frisco, the Mecca of all bums. We never saw a bum yet who hadn't been in 'Frisco or who didn't know all about the city.

Billy and me had heard about it, but hadn't seen it, and though we were on the tramp, didn't consider ourselves bums. We worked when we could find something to do, but when there was nothing to do, of course we couldn't do it. Work is something a bum will never do. Lots of the bums we met along the road were criminals and some of them pretty desperate ones at that. A few were chaps who were merely traveling to get somewhere and had no money to pay their way. Others had money and would not pay. Some were honest laboring men flitting from point to point in search of work, and not a few were unfortunates who had held high positions and were down and out through drink or misfortune of some sort. There were all sorts beating their way, and there always will be. The professional vag is a low down fellow who has few redeeming qualities. He is agreeable with his chums and that is about all. Neither Billy nor I were low, base born fellows, or criminals, and our parents were respectable, so that is why we took to each other. We were fellow mortals in distress, that is all. We did not think it very wrong to take a chicken if we were very hungry, but that was the extent of our evil doing. We bought our own clothes, blankets, etc., and never broke into a house to steal anything. One outfit that we were with at one time in Utah, one night stole a suit case that was standing on the platform of a railroad station and they divided up its contents among themselves. It consisted of a coat, vest, pants, collars, ties, handkerchiefs, brush, combs, etc., and had we been caught the whole bunch of us might have been pinched, but the gang made tracks in a hurry and got as far away from the scene of the robbery as they could. Some of the characters we met in our travels would have contaminated a saint almost, for their looks, actions and words revealed their disposition. The higher up in crime some of these chaps were, and the abler and more desperate, the more were they admired by some of their fellows. This kind of chaps were generally the captains of the camp, and gave orders that were readily obeyed by the others. One bum was generally commanded by the captain to go and rustle up bread, another was sent for meat, a third for coffee, a fourth for sugar, a fifth for pepper and salt, etc. No matter how things were obtained, if they were obtained no questions were asked.

One fellow returned to camp with a quarter of a lamb one night and boastfully told how he had got it. It had hung up outside a butcher shop and he stole it. The captain mumbled his approval in low tones, for he was too mighty to praise loudly or in many words.

The ways of hobos are various, and it would take up a great deal of space to describe them in detail.

It was along toward sundown when we made a train out of Davis. Davis, like Sacramento, was a pretty hard town to get out of, and the best we could do was to ride the rods. That was easy enough, even for Billy, who was rather delicate at that time. The rods under some freight cars are many and well arranged for riding purposes. They are fairly thick bars of iron set close together, stretching from one side of the car to the other, underneath the body of the car, and though not very often soft, when an overcoat is strung across them, with rolled up blankets for a pillow, they are the next best thing to a berth in a Pullman car. When one side of our body ached, we just turned over to the other side, and it beat riding on the bumpers or brake-beams all hollow. A berth in a Pullman costs about five dollars per night, fare extra, so we were saving lots of money. Beating our way on a railroad we considered no crime at all, for to judge from what I can read in the newspapers, the railroads rob the people, so why shouldn't the people rob them? That's a good argument, ain't it?

The measly old train must have been a way-freight, for she made long stops at every little excuse of a town she came to. About ten o'clock at night she came to a place called Benicia, and there the train was cut in two, so I hopped off to see what the difficulty was. On both sides and ahead of us was water. I rushed back to Billy and told him to get off in a hurry.

"What's the matter?" asked Billy.

"There's water all around us, and I guess they're going to carry the cars over on a ferry boat. I suppose our journey for the night will end here."

"Not much, Windy," replied Billy; "I want to get to 'Frisco tonight and maybe we can pay our way across on the boat."

We walked boldly on a boat that we saw the cars being pulled onto by a locomotive, and when we got near a cabin a ship's officer stepped up to us and wanted to know where we were going.

"To 'Frisco," said I.

"To 'Frisco?" said he with a grin. "Well, you'll have to pay your way across the ferry on this boat."

"What's the fare?" asked Billy.

"Seeing that you two are good-looking fellows, I'll only charge you ten cents apiece," said the captain, or officer, jokingly.

We both drew a long breath of relief, for we thought the boat was going to 'Frisco and that we'd have to pay a big price. I handed the good-natured officer two dimes for us both and we felt happy once more. The boat wasn't long making the trip, only about ten minutes or so, and on the other side we found no difficulty in making our train again, after she was made up. We held her down until she reached Oakland, which is opposite 'Frisco. There we learned there was one more ferry to cross before we could get into 'Frisco, so Billy and I decided to remain where we were for the night, for it was late. We prowled around until we found an open freight car, and turned in for a snooze.

The next morning was a beautiful one, and we were up and out by daylight. The weather wasn't cold, the sun was bright and cheery, but over 'Frisco we could see a sort of fog hanging. It was easy enough to see across the bay of San Francisco, for the distance is only about five miles, but the length of the bay we could not determine, for it stretched further than the eye could reach. We noticed an island in the bay not far from Oakland, and from Oakland a long wharf extended far out into the harbor, maybe a mile or so. We walked along this wharf until we came to a big train-shed and ferry house combined, where we coughed up two more dimes and got upon a large ferry-boat. As it was very early in the morning, very few passengers were on the boat. We walked to the front of the boat and drank in the delicious morning breeze. The ferry-boat was as large and fine a one as I had ever seen. It was a double-decker with large cabins below and aloft, and with runways for vehicles between. The cabins were very spacious and handsomely fitted up.

At about half past five the boat started on her way across, and now we were making a straight shoot for 'Frisco. Talking of 'Frisco, by the way, permit me to say a word about the name. The people of San Francisco don't like to have their city called 'Frisco, but prefer to have it called by its full title. They think the abbreviation is a slur. I can't see it in that light. 'Frisco is short and sweet and fills the bill; life is too short to call it San Francisco.

The ride across the bay was fine and lasted about half an hour. We passed an island which someone told us was Goat Island, and Billy and me wondered whether there were any billies or nannies on it. We didn't get close enough to see any. Further on we saw another island which was hilly like Goat Island. It was called Alcatraz. It contained an army post and was fortified. It looked formidable, we thought. Not very far away, and straight out, was the Golden Gate, which had no gates near it that we could see, but just two headlands about a mile or so apart. Outside of the Golden Gate is the Pacific Ocean.

We were now nearing 'Frisco, which lay right ahead of us. Nothing but steep hills could we see. They were built up compactly with houses. As we got close to the shore we saw plenty of level streets and wharves, and alongside of the wharves, ships. We steered straight for a tall tower on which there was a huge clock, which told us the time—six o'clock. We entered the ferry slip, moored fast and soon set foot in 'Frisco.

CHAPTER II.

'FRISCO.

Our first glimpse of 'Frisco made us like the place. Near the ferry slip were eating joints by the bushel, more saloons than you could shake a stick at, sailors' boarding houses, fruit stands containing fruit that made our teeth water; oyster-houses, lodging-houses—in fact there was everything there to make a fellow feel right at home. 'Frisco is all right and everyone who has been there will tell you so. What she ain't got ain't worth having. Every bum that I ever saw spoke well of the town and gave it a good name. It is a paradise for grafters. You can get as good a meal there for ten cents as you will have to pay double for anywhere else. Fruit is fine, plentiful and cheap; vegetables are enormous in size and don't cost anything, hardly; any and every kind of fish is there; meats are wonderful to behold, and not dear; and say, it's an all-around paradise, sure enough. Every kind of people can be found there—Greasers, Greeks, Scandinavians, Spanish, Turks, Armenians, Hebrews, Italians, Germans, Chinese, Japanese, negroes and all sorts. It is a vast international city.

Bums are there in unlimited quantities, any number of criminals, bunco-men, "chippies" till you can't rest, highbinders by the score up in Chinatown, and lots of bad people. The town is noted for being pretty lively. It surely is wide open and you can sit in a little game at any time. Californians in particular and Westerners generally take to gambling as naturally as a darky does to watermelons and pork chops. The 'Frisco gambling houses are never closed. Efforts have been made to close them but they were futile. Might as well try to sweep back the ocean with a broom. There are lots of good people in 'Frisco, but the bad ones are more than numerous. I think 'Frisco is about the liveliest, dizziest place on the continent to-day, of its size. It has more restaurants, saloons, theaters, dance halls, pull-in-and-drag-out places, groceries with saloon attachments to them, than any place I ever struck. Money is plentiful, easy to obtain and is spent lavishly. A dollar seems less to a Californian than a dime to an Easterner. He will let it go quicker and think less of it. If he goes into a restaurant or saloon and buys a drink or meal which does not suit him, he pays the price and makes no kick, but don't go there again. He don't believe in kicking. He was not brought up that way. He will lose his money at the races and try his luck again. "Better luck next time," says he, and his friends to him. He will take his girl out and blow in his money for her on the very best of everything. The best theater, the best wine supper are none too good for his girl. What if he does go broke, there's plenty more money to be had. Money is no object to a 'Friscoite. Billy and I weren't in 'Frisco long before we got onto these things.

Californians are sociable and will talk to anyone. Billy concluded to live and die there, the place suited him so well. Work was plentiful, wages were high, and the working hours few. Billy said it beat the old country all hollow. Ha'-pennies or tup-pennies didn't go here; the least money used was nickels and dimes. Nothing could be purchased for less than a nickel (five cents) for even a newspaper of any kind cost that much. No wonder the newsboys could shoot craps or play the races. Even the servant girls gambled in something or other. 'Frisco is all right. Bet your sweet life! The rest of America ain't in it with her. Lots of Britishers live there, too; that is why Billy liked it so well. Everyone who ain't sick or got the belly ache, or some other trouble, likes 'Frisco. As regards climate! They have it in 'Frisco. About sixty degrees by the thermometer all the year round. No snow, ice, cyclones or mosquitoes; but bed-bugs, fleas, earthquakes and fogs. As for fleas, they are thick in 'Frisco and mighty troublesome. When you see a lady or gent pinch his or her leg that means a bite—flea. As 'Frisco is built on a sandy peninsula, that may be the reason why fleas are so plentiful, for it is said they like sandy spots.

Billy and I had a little money which we earned in Sacramento, so we conclud-ed that the first thing to do was to get a square meal. We sought out a likely look-ing restaurant along the water front where a good meal could be had for ten cents and in we went. I ordered a steak and Billy ordered mutton chops; Billy wanted tea and I wanted coffee. Each of us had a bowl of mush first, then potatoes, bread and butter, hot cakes, tea or coffee, and meat. More than we could eat was put before us and I had a horse-like appetite. Billy was a little off his feed. The meal was as good as it was cheap. The next thing to be done was to hunt up a lodging place. There were any number of them in the vicinity, and we soon found a joint where the two of us could room together for a dollar and a half per week. The place was over a saloon, and though it wasn't high-toned, it seemed neat enough.

The next event on the program was sight-seeing. We left our things under lock and key in our room and leisurely strolled along the water front to see what we could see. While strolling along the street facing the wharves, we were passing a clothing store when a Hebrew gentleman stepped out and asked us if we wanted to buy a suit of clothes. We told him no, but he didn't seem to want to take "no" for an answer.

"Shentlemens, I got some mighty fine clothes inside and I'll sell them very cheap."

"Ain't got no money, today," said I, as we tried to pass on.

"Don't be in der hurry," said the Hebrew gentleman; "come in and take a look, it won't cost you noddings."

I was for moving on, but Billy said, "What's the harm? Let's go in and see what he's got."

In we went, slowly and cautiously, but we knew the old Jew couldn't rob us in open daylight.

"What size do you wear?" asked he of Billy.

"Damfino," says Billy; "I didn't come in to buy any clothes today."

"Let me measure you," says the Israelite, "I got some clothes here that will make your eyes water when you see dem."

Billy stood up and let his measure be taken. This done, the vender of clothes made an inspection of the clothing-piles, calling out to Jakie in a back room to come forth and assist. Jakie appeared, and seemed a husky chap of twenty-five or so. Jakie had been eating his breakfast. The two storekeepers went through the clothing piles.

"Aha!" triumphantly exclaimed the old Hebrew. "I've got a fine suit here. Dey'll make you look like a gentleman. Try 'em on," turning to Billy.

He brought forth the clothes where Billy could examine them, but after examination Billy shook his head.

"You don't like 'em?" exclaimed the old gent; "what's de matter with 'em?"

"Oh, I don't fancy that kind of cloth," said Billy.

It looked like gray blotting paper.

"What kind do you like?" asked the Hebrew, rather aggressively.

"Oh, I don't know," answered Billy.

The Jew was getting mad, but he brought forth another suit after a short search.

"Here is something fine; you kin wear 'em for efery day or Sunday."

Billy examined the clothes, but shook his head.

"Dry 'em on! Dry 'em on! You'll see they'll fid you like der paper on der vall!"

"What's the use trying 'em on?" said Billy, quietly; "I don't like 'em and they wouldn't fit me anyway."

"Not like 'em!" exclaimed the now thoroughly enraged clothing merchant; "I don't think you want to buy no clothes at all; you couldn't get a finer suit of clothes in San Francisco, and look at der price, too; only ten dollars, so hellup me Isaac!"

"The price is all right, but I don't like the cut of the clothes," said Billy.

"You don't like der style?"

The angry man now got the thought through his noddle that Billy wasn't going to buy any clothes, whereupon he grew furious.

"What you come in here for, you dirty tramp. Get out of here, or I trow you out."

Here I stepped up and told the miserable duffer what I thought of him. I expected there was going to be a knock down and drag out scene, but as there were two of us, the two Israelites thought better of it than to tackle us. The young feller hadn't said a word, but the old man was mad clear through. If he had been younger I would have swiped him one just for luck. We got out of the place all right, the old man and I telling each other pretty loud what we thought of each other. I told Billy he ought not to have gone in there at all for he didn't intend to buy any clothes.

"He wanted me to go in, didn't he, whether I wanted to or not?" asked Billy.

"Of course, he did. You should have given him a kick in the rump and skipped out. That's what I would have done."

"I'm glad it didn't end in a row. We might have got into trouble," concluded Billy.

We strolled along the wharves to see the shipping. The ferry-house at the foot of Market Street is a huge granite building (with a lofty clock-tower on top) wherein are to be found the various ticket offices of the Southern Pacific, Santa Fe, the North Shore, California & North Western and other railroads. Up stairs in the second story is an extensive horticultural exhibit, where are displayed the products of California; there are the offices of various railroad and other officials, there, too. To take a train on any railroad one must cross the bay on a ferry-boat. Each railroad line has its own line of ferry-boats and slips. One line of boats crosses to Oakland, Alameda and Berkeley; another to Tiburon; a third to Sausalito; a fourth to Point Richmond, etc. Every boat is a fine one and those of the Santa Fe Railroad plying to Point Richmond are all painted yellow. The traffic at the ferry building is considerable at all hours of the day and night.

The next wharf, which is also a covered one like the ferry-house, is the landing-place of the Stockton steamboats. There are two lines of these boats plying between 'Frisco and Stockton, and they are rivals. The distance between Stockton and 'Frisco by water is about one hundred miles, yet the fare is only fifty cents. There are sleeping berths aboard, if one cares to use them, at fifty cents each, and meals may be had for twenty-five cents. Fifty cents in Western lingo is called four bits, and twenty-five cents, two bits. A dime is a short bit and fifteen cents a long bit; six bits is seventy-five cents, and a dollar is simply called a dollar.

A few of the wharves we noticed were roofed over, but some were not. The Folsom Street Wharf is devoted to the United States Army transport service, and a huge transport ship going to Manila and other eastern countries can be seen there at any time, almost. No one is allowed on this wharf, except on business. As we hadn't any particular business on this wharf we didn't care to go upon it. There was a watchman at the gate. At a wharf or two from this one all the whaling vessels dock, and 'Frisco today is the greatest whaling port in America, we were told. There was one whaling vessel there at the time, but she didn't look good to us. She was short, squat, black and grimy, and smelled loudly of oil. Billy and I concluded we wouldn't care to sail in such a ship for a hundred dollars per month. Near by was a long uncovered wharf which extended quite a way out into the water. At either side of it were moored big deep-sea going vessels. One was the Dumbarton, of Glasgow, another the Selkirk, a third the Necker—all foreigners. The Selkirk was British, and Billy's heart warmed to her. When he saw an English flag flying on one of the masts tears came to his eyes and he got homesick. He walked up the gang-plank and wanted to go on board, but a sailor on deck told him there was no admittance. Billy marched down again much crestfallen. There are lots of evil characters in 'Frisco, so that is why the mariners are wary.

We slowly sauntered along the wharf, and at a string piece at the end of it we came across other idlers, several of whom were engaged in fishing. We saw several young sharks pulled up and several other kinds of fish that we didn't know the names of. After watching the fishing for a while we moved on and went into some of the side streets. They were full of saloons, some of which were fitted up very handsomely with plate-glass, fine woodwork, marble floors and elaborate bars with free lunch counter. Other saloons were mere groggeries in which we could see and hear sailors and longshoremen singing and dancing. Steam beer and lager was five cents a glass and whiskey ten cents. Sailors' boarding-houses were numerous in these localities, as were hotels, stores of all kinds, ship-outfitting shops, lumber yards, coal offices, foundries, iron works and the like.

We now strolled up Market Street, which is the main thoroughfare of 'Frisco. It is a broad street, flanked on either side by wholesale and retail commercial establishments, high-toned saloons and restaurants. Many street car lines traverse this street by means of cables, and there are one or two horse-car lines.

The street was a lively one, and thronged with people and vehicles. Billy and I had heard a great deal about the Golden Gate Park, the Cliff House, the Seal Rocks and the Sutro Baths, so we concluded to take a little jaunt out that way to see what those places were like.

The first things we wanted to see were the seals.

We boarded a street-car running out to the Cliff House, and found the ride a long and interesting one. The distance was many miles and the fare only five cents. There was much to be seen. Long stretches of unfamiliar streets rolled by, residence and business sections, strange looking houses, hills and valleys, and the like. The air was wonderfully balmy and bracing and not a bit cold. The car whirled us along very rapidly and revealed to us a great deal of Golden Gate Park, and further on lofty tree-covered hills, bare sand hills, and a very extensive public building of some sort which was perched on a tree clad hillside, and then it skimmed along parallel with the ocean. We saw no ships on the ocean, but it was a grand sight nevertheless. We rushed by a life-saving station at railroad speed, which we regretted, for we should like to have seen more of it, and after riding about a mile or so more, finally stopped alongside a shed, which was the end of the car line. Here we hopped off with the rest of the crowd, and walked along a wooden sidewalk which was laid over the sands. Two or three restaurants and saloons were to be seen in the vicinity, and about a half dozen booths. There was a picture gallery or two, and fruit and peanut stands.

We bought some candy and peanuts to keep from getting hungry, and then followed the crowd to the beach. We walked along the beach and then up a hill leading to the Cliff House. The views along this road were fine. We came to the Cliff House and saw it was nothing more nor less than a large hotel built on a cliff. It looked pretty high-toned to us, so me and Billy hesitated about going in.

"They'll soak us when we get in there, Windy," warned Billy.

"Nary time, Billy," retorted I. "We'll go in and if they try to hold us up we'll skip."

"All right, then; let's try our luck," said Billy.

In we went, and saw a barroom, which we didn't enter. Further on was a glass covered porch, along which were disposed tables and chairs, and which invited us to sit down and have something. We were not hungry or thirsty just then, so we kept a-walking, and through an open window facing the sea we saw some tall rocks in the water, about a quarter of a mile distant, upon which were a whole lot of seals that were barking to beat the band.

"There's the seals, Billy, large as life, sure enough," remarked I. Billy stared.

"I'll be blowed if they ain't cheeky beggars," said he, with a face full of astonishment. "It's a wonder they'd come so near to the shore."

Some of the animals were snoozing on the rocks, others were crawling up the rocky sides of the islet, a few were bellowing, and the whole place seemed covered with them. A wonderful sight it was! We looked until we grew tired, and I wanted to drag Billy away, but he didn't seem to want to go.

"There's other things to be seen, Billy," said I; "we can't stay here all day."

Billy tore himself away reluctantly and then we wandered over to the Sutro Heights, which is a tall hill with fine and extensive gardens upon it. From this hill a fine view of the ocean may be obtained. There are fine drives in these gardens bordered with flowers, shady walks, statues, fountains, rustic arbors and seats, cosy niches where one could sit and view the ocean, roads built terrace-like upon the cliffs, and other very pretty features. A lovely spot indeed, it was. It was built by Mr. Adolph Sutro, a millionaire. It was free to all. We walked in the gardens until we grew tired, and then sat down and contemplated the ocean. Afterward we strolled toward Golden Gate Park and inspected it. It was close by and we found it a very extensive one. It seemed endless, indeed, to us, for long before we reached an entrance where we could take a car, we were dead tired. We took another route going cityward, for we wanted to see as much of the city as we could. The more we saw of 'Frisco, the better we liked it. It must be seen to be appreciated. We reached Market Street all right, and then we knew where we were. We strolled down toward the ferry-house, near which we knew our lodging-house to be, and after having a good supper, we went to our room to lay off until evening, when there would be more sight-seeing.

"What do you think of 'Frisco, Windy?" asked Billy.

"Suits me to a T, Billy. Believe I'll camp here for a while."

"Same here, Windy. I never struck a place I like better. I think a fellow can get on here. I'm going to try it, anyway."

"I'm with you, Billy," said I. "Where'll we go this evening?"

"I've heard a lot about Chiney town. Suppose we go there."

"Good idea! Let's take it in."

Accordingly, about eight o'clock that evening we strolled forth, bent on seeing 'Frisco by gaslight. The streets were well lighted, and we found no difficulty in moving about. By making inquiries we readily found our way to the Mongolian district. What we saw there filled us with amazement. Street after street we saw (and long ones at that) inhabited solely by slanty-eyed Asiatics. There were thousands of them, and it seemed to us that we were transplanted into a Chinese city. All kinds of Chinese establishments were located in this quarter; barber shops, drug stores, furnishing goods stores, butcher shops, cigar manufacturing establishments, restaurants (chop suey), temples, theaters, opium joints in back alleys and basements, street venders who sold fruits, street cobblers, open air fortune tellers, newspapers, bookbinderies, vegetable stores, and not a few high-class curio establishments. Any number of Chinese children were noisily playing in the streets, Chinese women were walking about the streets and all over the quarter was an oriental atmosphere. It made us feel mighty foreign-like. Billy wanted to know whether he was in Asia or America, and I told him Asia. The Chinese women and children interested us considerably. The women were habited in loose flowing robes and trousers, and their lips and faces were painted scarlet. Their hair was done up in thick folds, with long golden pins stuck through them. They were mighty gaudy, I thought. The kids were noisy but interesting. They played all kinds of games like white children. Of course the games they played were Chinese, and what kind of games they were, I don't know. The articles of food and wear displayed were very curious. So were the books, photographs, etc.

Billy and I took in the sights, and felt mighty interested in it all. It was better than a circus to us. At about ten o'clock we meandered homeward.

We talked late that night about what we had seen, and it was after midnight before we fell asleep. Billy was unaccountably restless that night and kept a-tossing and a-rolling. He kept this up so long that finally I got huffy and asked him what the trouble was. He kept quiet for a while but suddenly he rose up and said he'd be — — if he didn't think there were bugs in the bed. I felt a bite or two myself, but didn't mind it.

"I'm going to get up and see what's in this bed," said Billy.

He got up, lit a candle, and I hopped out too, so as to give him a chance to examine things. Billy threw back the clothes and saw three or four good-sized fleas hopping about and trying to escape to a safe shelter. We both went for them bodily, but they were too swift for us. We did a pile of cussing and swearing just then, but the fleas were probably laughing at us from some safe retreat. We couldn't catch a one of them. We went to bed again and I slept soundly, but Billy put in a bad night. I told Billy the next morning he oughtn't to mind such trifling things as fleas.

"Trifles, are they?" snorted he, and showed me his bare white skin, which was all eaten up. "Look at that; call them trifles?"

"What are you going to do about it, Billy?" inquired I.

"Do?" retorted he, with disgust, "why, grin and bear it, of course; what else can I do; but those bites itch like blazes."

Billy had to do what all 'Frisco people do when they are bitten—grin and bear it, or cuss and scratch. The 'Frisco fleas sure are lively, and the best way to catch them is to wet your finger and bear down on them suddenly. They'll wiggle away from a dry finger.

The next morning was a fine one, balmy and sunny. We arose, dressed, breakfasted, and then felt happy.

"How are we going to put in the day, Windy?" asked Billy, after we emerged from a restaurant and stood picking our teeth in front of the place.

"Blest if I know," responded I. "Suppose we put it in sight-seeing?"

"I'll go you," said Billy. "We haven't seen much of 'Frisco yet. Suppose we take a stroll up Market Street and see what there is to see up that way."

Accordingly, up Market Street we leisurely strolled, taking in the sights by the wayside.

Market Street, as I said before, is the main thoroughfare of 'Frisco, and is a broad one. The sidewalks are wide enough for a dozen or more people to walk abreast along them and the driveway in the middle of the street contains two or three sets of street-car tracks, and sufficient room on either side for vehicles. The lower portion of the street, toward the ferry-house, is taken up with wholesale business establishments, and the upper portion toward which we were now walking contains retail shops, high-class saloons, restaurants, newspaper buildings, sky-scrapers, banks, department stores, etc. We came to Market and Third Street, and turned down Third Street. It, too, was rather a broad thoroughfare, but not nearly so wide as Market Street. It wasn't high-toned like Market Street, nor were the buildings on it of a high class, for they were mostly of frame, one and two stories in height. The ground floors of these buildings were used as stores and the upper portions as dwellings. Fruit, fish and vegetable stores abounded, and saloons were more than numerous. The size and varieties of the fruit, fish and vegetables in the stores pleased the eye. Fine crabs and clams were there, but the California oysters seemed small. We stepped into a saloon called "The Whale," where a fine free lunch was set out on a side table. There were huge dishes of cheese on the table, tripe, various kinds of sausage sliced up thin, pickled tongue, radishes, cold slaw, pickles, sliced tomatoes and big trays of bread of various kinds. The layout was generous. Having had breakfast but a short time before, all these dainties did not tempt us, but we sat down for awhile and indulged in a smoke, in the meanwhile observing the ways of the patrons of the place. Some seedy looking bums were lined up against the bar chinning whilst others were sipping beer and paying their best respects to the lunch counter. They were a dirty lot, and if some of them weren't hobos, I miss my guess. We didn't remain in the place long, but strolled into a similar establishment further on. In one saloon we noticed a sign over the lunch counter which informed the hungry one to—

"Please regulate your appetite according to your thirst; this is not a restaurant."

Notwithstanding the gentle hint conveyed on the sign, the place did a roaring trade, for the liquids as well as the solids were excellent.

Beginning from Market and running parallel with Market were Mission, Howard, Folsom, Bryant, Brannan, Bluxome, Townsend, Channel and other streets. Nearly all of them were broad, but a few were narrow, such as Stevenson, Jessie, Minna, Natoma, Tehama, etc., being hardly more than alleys. This was the poorer residence section, inhabited by the working classes. Some of the alleys were tough and contained cheap lodging-houses wherein dwelt many a hard case and criminal.

We walked down Third Street as far as the railroad depot and saw lots of things to interest us. All the goods displayed in the store windows seemed dirt cheap. How they did tempt us, but as we were not overburdened with wealth just then we didn't feel like buying. Silk pocket handkerchiefs, dandy hats, elegant trousers, mouth harmonicas, pistols, knives, razors, accordions were there in great variety. Why were we born poor? Had we been rich we would have blowed ourselves for fair. The display was too tempting. We walked to Fourth Street, which is the next one to Third, and then slowly sauntered up toward Market again. The blocks along Third and Fourth Streets were long ones, and from Market Street down to the railroad depot the distance is a mile or more. But we were not tired, so on we kept. Fourth Street was about like Third Street, and afforded many interesting sights. Billy and me liked everything we saw. When we finally reached Market Street again we crossed it and took in another quarter of the city. Where we had been was called south of Market; so this must be north of Market. We didn't like it half as well as we did south of Market. Here were pretentious shops and restaurants, and a fine class of dwellings, but even here the buildings were all of wood and hardly two were alike. In this quarter is located what is called "The Tenderloin," which means gambling joints, fast houses and the like. We, being strangers, could not locate them. It was now nearing noon and as we had become hungry, we concluded to step into a saloon to have a beer and a free lunch, but the free lunch establishments in that neighborhood seemed few and far between. Some saloons had signs on them which stated that free clam chowder, beef stew, roasted clams, or a ham sandwich with every drink was to be had today, but those were not the kind of a place we were after. We were looking for some place like "The Whale," but couldn't find one. We finally got tired of hunting for such a place, and stepped into a ten-cent restaurant, where we had a bum meal. After dining we strolled back to our lodging-house, where we laid off the rest of the day.

"What'll it be tonight; a ten-cent show or Chinatown once more?"

"A ten-cent show," answered Billy; "we did Chinatown last night, and can do it again some other night, so let's take in a show."

Accordingly we went to a fine big theater that evening where the prices ranged from ten to fifty cents, and went up to "nigger heaven" (price ten cents), from whence we saw a pretty fair variety show. The show consisted of singing, dancing, moving pictures, a vaudeville play, negro act, monologue speaker and an acrobatic act. The performance lasted about two hours. The negro act made Billy laugh until he nearly grew sick, and we both enjoyed ourselves hugely. One singer, an Australian gentleman, sang the "Holy City," and he sang it so well that he was recalled many times. The little vaudeville play was good, and so were the moving pictures. It was about ten o'clock when the play let out, and it was after midnight when Billy and I turned in.

We continued our sightseeing tour about a week and saw about all worth seeing of 'Frisco, and then as funds began to run low, we concluded it was about time for us to look for work. I struck a job as helper in a foundry the very next day, but Billy was not so fortunate. He did not find a job for several days. Of course I went "snucks" with him when he wasn't working, and saw to it that he had a bed to sleep in and something to eat, for he would have done as much for me.

Billy struck a job a few days afterward and it was one that seemed to please him mightily. It was in a swell hotel run by an Englishman and Billy was installed as pantryman. His duties were to take good care of and clean the glassware and silverware. The job was an easy one, with the pay fairly good. Billy said it was like getting money from home. He worked from seven o'clock in the morning until eight at night, and had three hours off in the afternoon. The waiters took a shine to him, for they, like himself, were English, and brought him all kinds of good things to eat in the pantry, which was his headquarters.

They brought him oysters, roast fowl of various kinds, game, ice cream, water ices, plum pudding, the choicest of wines, etc., and were sociable enough to help Billy eat and drink these things. No one molested them so long as they did their work, for the cast-off victuals would have gone into the swill-barrel, anyway. Billy was in clover and had the best opportunity in the world to grow stout on "the fat of the land." I was glad to know that he was getting along so well for he sure was a true and steady little pard.

One night, several weeks after this, when we were in our room chinning, I remarked to Billy: "Say, Billy, you have told me so much about the old country that I've a notion to go there."

Billy looked at me keenly to see if I was joking, but I wasn't. "I mean it, Billy," said I. "I've always had a notion that I'd like to see the old country, and if you can get along here I guess I can get along over there."

"You're way off, Windy," replied Billy, "the old country is different from this, in every way."

"In what way."

"Why, you can't beat your way over there as you can here, and you couldn't earn as much there in a week as you can here in a day. And the ways of people are different, too. Stay where you are, Windy; that's my advice to you."

"You say I can't beat my way in the old country, Billy; why not?" asked I.

"You'll get pinched the first thing, if you try it. In the first place there are no railroad trains running across to Europe, so how are you going to cross the little duck pond; swim across?"

"How do others cross it; can't I ride over in a boat?"

"Of course you can but it will cost you lots of money, and where are you going to get it?"

"What's the matter with earning it or getting a job on a steamer; didn't you do it?"

"Of course I did; but the steamship companies hire their help on the other side of the ocean, not on this side."

"Go on, Billy; you are giving me a fairy tale."

"No, I'm not," earnestly responded Billy; "it's true as preaching."

I doubted just the same.

"You say I can't beat my way when I get across to Europe; why not?"

"Because they won't let you. The towns are close together, for the country is small, and if you beat your way on a train you'd be spotted before you traveled ten miles. And another thing, there are no brake-beams on the other side, no blind baggage and no bumpers, so where are you going to ride? And another thing, too; the railway cars over there are totally different from those here. The coaches are different, the engines are different, the freight cars are different; everything is so different," said Billy with a reminiscent smile.

"Go on, Billy; you're only talking to hear yourself talk," said I, thinking he was romancing.

"You say, Billy," continued I, "that the ways of the people are different over there; in what way?"

"In every way. I couldn't begin to explain it all to you, if I tried six months."

"They talk English over there, don't they? Can't I talk English?"

"Of course you can," laughed Billy; "but their language is different from yours and so are their ways. Their victuals are different; their dress, their politics—"

"Cut out the politics, Billy; I ain't going over there to run for office. They must be a queer lot on the other side of the pond to judge from what you say."

"Not a bit queer," warmly responded Billy. "They are just different, that is all. We will suppose you are over there, Windy. What will you do?"

"Do the Britishers, of course; what else?"

"Better stay at home and do your own countrymen. You'll find it easier," gravely admonished Billy. "You are on your own ground and know the country and the ways of the people. You'd have a hard time of it over there; mind now, I'm giving it to you straight. I don't think you're serious about going."

"Serious and sober as a judge, Billy. I've been thinking about this thing for a long time. Let me tell you something else, Billy, that I haven't told you before. I intend to keep a diary when I get on the other side and write down everything I see worth noting."

"The hell you are," profanely responded Billy; "what are you going to do with it after it is written down?"

"Have it printed in a book," calmly responded I.

Billy regarded me intently, as a dog does a human being whom he is trying to understand and cannot, and then when the full force of my revelation struck him he dropped on the bed and laughed and laughed until I thought he'd split his sides.

"What's tickling you, Billy?" asked I, grinning, for his antics made me laugh.

"You—you—" here he went off into another fit. "*You* write a book? Say, Windy, I've been traveling with you a long while but I never suspected you were touched in the upper story."

"No more touched than you are, Billy," said I indignantly. Billy rose up.

"So you're going to write a book, eh?" asked Billy, still laughing. "Do you know anything about grammar, geography or composition?"

"You bet I do, Billy; I was pretty fair at composition when I was at school, but I always hated grammar and don't know much about it."

"That settles it," said Billy. "How could you write a book if you don't know anything about grammar?"

"That stumps me, Billy, but I guess the printer can help me out."

"The printer ain't paid for doing that sort of thing; he won't help you out."

"The h—— he won't," responded I, angrily; "that's what he's paid for, isn't it?"

"I don't think," said Billy. "Say, Windy, you're clean off. Better turn in and sleep over it."

"Sleep over nothing," quickly retorted I; "am I the first man who ever wrote a book?"

"No, you ain't the first, nor the last damn fool who has tried it."

"Now, see here, Billy," said I, getting heated, "let me tell you something. I've read a whole lot of books in my time, and a good many of them weren't worth hell room. I've read detective stories that were written by fellows that didn't know anything about the detective business. Look at all the blood-and-thunder novels will you, that are turned out every year by the hundred. Not a word in them is true, yet lots of people read them. Why? Because they like them. See what kids read, will you? All about cowboys, Indians, scalping, buffalo hunting, the Wild West, etc. After the kids read such books they get loony and want to go on scalping expeditions themselves, so they steal money, run away from home, buy scalping knives, pistols and ammunition, and play hell generally. My book ain't that kind. When I write a book it will contain the truth, the whole truth and nothing but the truth."

"So help you ——," irreverently put in Billy.

"No foolishness, Billy; I'm serious."

"Oh, you are, are you?" answered Billy; "well, let's hear something serious, then."

"Did you ever read the life of the James boys, Billy?"

"No, I never did? Who were they?"

"They were outlaws and robbers, and the book I read about them was the most interesting one I ever read. It was all facts, solid facts, and no nonsense about it. That's what I want to write, solid facts."

"About the James boys?"

"No, you little ignoramus; about what I see in the old country."

"There are many smarter men than you are that have written books about the old country, Windy, and some of these writers were English and some were American. Are you going to go in opposition to them?"

"Opposition your grandmother! Haven't I got as good a right to write a book as anyone else?"

"Who says you haven't? After you get the book printed who's going to sell it for you; going around peddling it?"

"No, I expect the printer to print what I write, and buy the book from me."

"Who gets all the money from the sale of the book?" asked Billy, with a huge grin on his face.

"Why, I expect that the printer and me'll go snucks. He gets half for printing it, and I get half for writing it."

"Oh, that's the game, is it? I think you'll have a sweet time of it finding a printer on that sort of a deal."

"Don't you think that would be a fair divvy?"

"No, the printer is taking all the chances and you're taking none. He puts up the dough and what do you put up?"

"My time and ability."

"Your *ability*!" shouted Billy as he went off into a spasm; "well, you've got lots of time, but I never know'd you had any ability."

"Laugh away, old boy," said I, considerably nettled; "it takes ability to write a book."

"Of course it does," said Billy, meaningly.

"Maybe you think I ain't got any?"

"Maybe you have, but you'll have to show me."

"Well, Billy," said I, "we've discussed this matter long enough; suppose we go to bed."

Nothing more was said on the subject that night. The next morning we went to our separate jobs as usual, and I did a good deal of thinking during the day over some of the information Billy had given me about the old country. It made me waver at times about going, but at other times it did not. That night, after we came home from work, Billy and me took a stroll as usual through Chinatown, and every time we went through it we found something new to see. The streets were always thronged with celestials and sightseers, the stores of the Chinese and Japanese were all lit up, the queer goods in the windows still riveted our attention and the ways of the orientals proved a source of never-ending interest to us. There were several Chinese theaters in the quarter, too, in which the beating of gongs and the "high-toned" singing could plainly be heard by us, but as the admission fees to these theaters to the "Melican man" was fifty cents, we didn't go in. Some of the plays lasted about six weeks.

We were strolling along quietly enjoying ourselves, when suddenly Billy banteringly remarked: "By the way, Windy, when are you going to take that little flier across the duck-pond?"

"Don't know, Billy; haven't decided yet."

"What are you going to do with all the money you make out of that book of yourn?"

"Never you mind, Billy; I'm going to write the book just the same; don't you worry about that."

"I suppose you'll get rich some day, and cut me the first thing. Fellers who write books make lots of money. I suppose you'll buy a mansion on Nob Hill, have a coach and four with a coachman in livery on the box and the regulation flunkey behind. Maybe you'll drive tandem and handle the ribbons yourself?"

"Stop roasting me, Billy; let up!"

But Billy continued mercilessly; "Of course you'll have a box at the opera, wear a claw hammer coat and a plug hat, put on white kids and take your lady-love to a little supper after the play is over. Be lots of champagne flowing about that time, eh?"

"Let up, you darned little Britisher," said I laughing. "Greater things than that have come to pass. I'll cut you, the first thing, Billy."

"I knew it. Rich people ain't got any use for their poor friends or relations.

"Which bank will you put your money in?"

"Haven't decided yet; ain't going to let that worry me."

"Maybe you'll fall in love with some girl and get married. When a feller has money he'll do fool things."

"The girl I marry will have to be a pretty good looker, and will have to have a little money of her own," responded I.

"Of course, Windy; I'm glad to see you've got some sense. After that old country trip yarn of yours I didn't think you had any."

"No yarn about it, Billy; I'm going."

"Where to?"

"To the old country."

"When?"

"Oh, you're asking me too many questions. Better go to the old country with me, Billy."

"Not I, Windy; I've been there and know what it is. I'll never return to it until I'm rich."

"Hope that'll be soon, Billy."

"So do I, Windy; but it don't look that way now."

"Can you blame me for trying to make a stake?" asked I.

"Blame you, no; but you'll never make a stake writing a book."

"Faint heart never won a fair lady, my boy, and I'm going to try it, if it takes a leg off."

"I believe you are serious, Windy; I thought you were kiddin'!"

"Kiddin' nothing; I was serious from the go-off."

"Well, Windy, old pard, I wish you luck but it don't look to me as if you'd make it. Too big a contract."

"Time will tell."

We had many another talk on the subject, Billy bantering me every time, for he either couldn't or wouldn't believe I was serious. We had been together so long, that he was loath to believe I would desert him.

One evening when I came home from work I informed Billy that I had made up my mind positively to start out on my trip at the end of the week. You should have seen him when I told him this. At first he argued, then, seeing that did no good, he called me all kinds of a fool, and cursed and fumed. He finally told me to go to hades if I wished, for he had no strings on me. He didn't care a tinker's damn how soon I went, or what became of me. He hoped I'd get drowned, or, if not that, then pinched as soon as I set foot on British soil. The little fellow was badly wrought up. I informed him it was my intention to beat my way to New York and that when I got that far, I would plan the next move. I told him also that I didn't believe in crossing a river until I got to it, and that I would find some means of crossing the ocean. He sarcastically advised me again to swim across, but I took no heed. We parted the next morning and I knew Billy felt sore, but he didn't show it. He told me that he should remain in 'Frisco, and that I would find him there when I came back, that is, if I ever came back.

"Oh, I'll come back, my boy; never fear."

"And mind what I told you about my folks. If you go to London they live only a short way from there, and if you see them tell them all about me."

"I'll do it, old pard, and write you everything," responded I.

"Good-bye, then, Windy, and don't take in any bad money while you're gone," was Billy's parting bit of advice.

I felt bad, too, but didn't show it. I was leaving the true-heartedest little fellow that ever lived, but the best of friends must part sometimes.

CHAPTER III.
THE JOURNEY OVERLAND.

The distance from 'Frisco to New York overland, is over three thousand miles, and by water it is much more than that, but such little trips are a trifle to me, as they are to every well-conditioned wayfarer. I started out happily enough one fine day at dawn to make the long journey and though I did feel a qualm or two the first few days after leaving Billy, the feeling soon wore off. I chose the central route, which is the shortest via Sacramento, Reno, Ogden, Omaha, Chicago, Niagara Falls and New York, and I anticipated having lots of fun along the way. I was out for sight-seeing and adventure and believed I would have a good time. I didn't have any money to speak of, for, though I had worked several months I had saved nothing. Anyway, it wasn't safe to travel hobo style with money, for if anyone suspects you have any, it may be possible that you'll get knocked on the head or murdered outright for it. Such things are a common occurrence.

I got as far as Sacramento in good shape and when the freight train I was riding on got to Newcastle, which is a town in the foothills of the Sierra mountains, a long halt was made to attach a number of refrigerator cars to it. These cars were laden with fruit. Had I wished I could have crawled into one of them and made the journey east in ten days, or less, for they are laden with perishable goods and travel as fast, almost, as a passenger train, but I didn't care to travel that way, for the reason that I didn't like it. These refrigerator cars have heavy air-tight doors at the sides which are hermetically sealed when the cars are loaded, making the cars as dark as a pocket. When in them one can't see anything and can hardly turn around. There are no conveniences whatever. One must take a sufficiency of supplies with him to last during the trip in the shape of food and water, and one must go unwashed and unkempt during the journey. Lots of hobos travel that way, and think nothing of it, but I didn't care to do so. It is almost as bad, if not worse, than being in jail, for one can take little or no exercise, and the only light and ventilation afforded is from the roof, where there is an aperture about two feet wide, over which there is a sliding door. This can be shoved up or down, but it is usually locked when the train is en route. The cars must be kept at an even temperature always, and must not be too hot or too cold. A certain number of tons of ice is put into a compartment at either end of the car, which keeps the temperature even. The side doors, as I said, are hermetically closed and sealed. Thus the fruits, meats, vegetables or whatever the car may contain, are kept fresh and sweet. I slipped into one of these loaded cars and had a look around, but one survey was enough for me. I didn't like the prospect at all. Ten days of imprisonment was too much.

Any hobo may ride over the Sierra Nevada Mountains as far as Reno without being molested, for it is a rule of the Southern Pacific Railroad Company not to incur their ill-will. Some hobos have been known to set fire to the snow sheds in revenge for being put off a train in the lonely mountains. Fires occur in the snow-sheds every year, but of course it is hard to tell who or what starts a fire. The sheds are of wood and have always had to be rebuilt, for without them the road would be blocked every winter and traffic stopped. There are miles of them and wonderful creations they are. They are roofed over and very strongly built.

I held down the freight train until we reached Reno, where I was glad to hop off for rest and refreshment. Refreshments of all kinds are plentiful in Reno. The railroad runs through the main street of the town and the town is a wide open one. Across the track along the main street are restaurants, saloons and gambling houses. The gambling is not done secretly for it is licensed and anyone may play who wishes. One may step into, at least, one of these places from the street, for the gambling room is on the ground floor. It is a handsomely appointed apartment. The floors are of marble, the drinking bar is elaborate, the fittings superb. In front, as you enter, is the bar and behind it a back bar with the finest of glassware. The liquors are of excellent quality. Opposite the bar, near the wall, are faro and crap tables. At the rear of the long apartment is a horseshoe shaped lunch counter, where the best the market affords can be had at reasonable rates. The bar and restaurant are patronized by gamblers and by outsiders who never gamble. Anyone over the age of twenty-one may step inside and play, and no questions are asked. The crap game is interesting. It is played with dice and anyone may throw the dice. The way some fellows throw them would make a horse laugh. Some throw them with a running fire of conversation, their eyes blazing with excitement. Others, like the coons, keep a saying as they throw the dice, "Come seben, come eleben!" "What you doin' dar?" "Roll right dis time for me you son of—" etc., etc. It is interesting to watch the players. Many refined men visit these places and sometimes take a little flyer. These men are quiet, open-handed fellows, who seem to regard their little indulgence in the play as a joke, whether they win or lose. They seem to have plenty of money and don't care—at least one would judge so from their manner. While observing them I thought it must be a fine thing to have plenty of money, so as not to care whether you win or lose.

Westerners, as a rule, are free and generous, and seem to be just as ready to spend their money as they are to earn it.

Bootblacks, waiters, cooks, newsboys and all sorts of men are always ready and willing to take a chance in the games. Sometimes they win and sometimes they lose, but win or lose they are always ready to try their luck again.

Another gaming place I went into was situated on the first floor above the street in a building facing the railroad, and it, too, was palatial. On the ground floor was the saloon and above were the gambling rooms. A pretty tough crowd was in them at the time of my visit and the crowd was so dense it was rather difficult to move about. I was jostled considerably and found it difficult to get near the gaming tables. Craps and roulette were the main games here, too.

Fights and shooting scrapes are common in the gambling places, but the Reno officers are alert and fearless, and soon put obstreperous people where the dogs won't bite them.

Notwithstanding its gambling and recklessness, Reno is a good business town, and full of orderly, respectable people. There are many wholesale and retail establishments in the town; ice plants, machine shops, breweries, ore reduction works and lumber yards. Besides, it is a great cattle shipping center.

Many of the streets are broad and well-shaded, and the Truckee River, in which are any number of speckled beauties in the shape of mountain trout, flows through the town. Surrounding Reno are tall mountains which form a part of the Sierra Nevada range, but they seem bare and lonely.

I landed in Reno during the afternoon and steered straight for the Truckee River, as I needed a bath. I quickly espied a sequestered nook under a wagon-bridge on the outskirts of the town, and from the looks of things in the vicinity could tell that it was a hobo camping place. Old tin cans were strewn about, and down the bank near the water was a fireplace made of stones. One lone Wandering Willie was in camp and he greeted me as effusively as if I were a long-lost brother. A hobo can tell another hobo at a glance.

"Hello, pardner; how's tricks?" was the greeting of my fellow wayfarer.

"Fair to middlin'," responded I.

"Where you bound for?"

"Just got to Reno; and I am going to hold the town down for a while," said I. I was cautious and didn't want this chance acquaintance to know too much about my affairs.

"Where'd you come from?" inquired I.

"Me? Oh, I've been hittin' the line all the way from Bloomington, Illinoi', and I'm going to take a flier to the Coast."

"You are, hey? I just came from there."

"The hell you did; how's things out that way?"

"Fine and dandy; ever been there?"

"No," laconically answered the chap and began to question me about the Coast.

I gave him all the information I could and then told him I was going to take a wash-down. He had just done the same and as he seemed anxious to go to town he soon left me. I stripped and had a glorious bath in the cool, swift-flowing river. The river was neither broad nor very deep but so clear that I could see every stone at the bottom of it. Not a fish could I see but doubtless they were plentiful. After the clean-up I leisurely strolled along the railroad track into town and steered for a restaurant, where I had a good supper for twenty-five cents. I then lit my pipe and strolled about taking in the sights.

I remained in Reno a day or two, and did not find time hanging heavy on my hands. There are extensive cattle corrals about half a mile from the town where I put in a whole afternoon watching the loading of cattle into cars.

It was better than seeing a circus. A chute ran from the corral to the car to be loaded and the animals were made to walk the plank in great shape. No harm was done them unless they grew obstreperous, in which case there was a great deal of tail twisting done, punching in the ribs with long poles, yelling and shouting, which soon brought a refractory animal to terms.

The railroad depot in Reno is a lively spot, too.

The S. P. R. R. trains and the Virginia & Truckee Railroad use the same depot, and at train times there is always a sizeable crowd on hand. The Virginia & Truckee road, which goes from Reno to Virginia City, a distance of about sixty miles, is said to be the crookedest road in the country. It winds around bare mountain sides to a great height and is continually going upward. It was built in the early Bonanza mining days when times were flush and is said to have cost a lot of money. It has paid for itself many times over and was a great help to Gold Hill, Carson and Virginia City. Although it has been in existence over a quarter of a century and though it winds over almost inaccessible mountain peaks, not a human life up to the writing of this book (1907) has ever been lost on this road.

Indians may ride on the road free, and as they are aware of the fact, hardly a day passes but they may be seen in the smoking car or on the platform of a car taking a little flier to Carson, Virginia City, Washoe, Steamboat Springs or any other place along the line they care to go to. There is a State law in Nevada which permits any Indian to ride free on any railroad. What the object of this law is, I don't know.

I noticed that the passenger trains going eastward over the S. P. R. R. leave Reno between eight and nine o'clock at night, so I concluded to beat my way out of town on one of them. I noticed that others did it and that it was easy. All a fellow had to do was to let the train get a good move on, then swing underneath to the rods, or jump the blind baggage.

"The blind baggage is good enough for you, Windy," says I to myself. Accordingly, one very fine evening I permitted a passenger train to get a good move on, and then boarded her a little way out, before she began to go too fast. I was onto my job pretty well. I made it all right, but as soon as I swung onto the steps of the blind baggage I found I wasn't the only pebble on the beach for a number of other non-paying passengers were there who must have got on before the train pulled out. There were just seven deadheads on the car, excluding myself, and they were not a bit glad to see me. Seven on the platform of a car is a good many, but eight is one too many; so my fellow voyagers assured me by black looks. They were greasers, every one of them, and cow punchers at that, most likely. I was an American. There was no welcome for me. The greasers jabbered among themselves about me, but what they said I could not understand, for I don't understand Spanish.

Finally one of them said to me in fairly good English: "It's too much crowded here; you better jump off."

"Jump off while the train is going like this; not much! Jump off yourself and see how you like it," said I angrily.

Not only was I angry but apprehensive, for I felt there was going to be trouble. I was not armed and had only a pocket knife with me. Even had I been armed what could I have done against seven men in close quarters? Nothing was said to me for quite a while after that and the train clattered along at a great rate.

The cold, swift-rushing night wind blew keenly against us, making the teeth of some of the greasers chatter. They could stand any amount of heat but a little cold made them feel like hunting their holes. After riding along for an hour or so through the bare, cheerless plains of Nevada, the engine whistle blew for the town. The cow-puncher who had addressed me before spoke up and said: "It is more better you get off at the next station."

"No, I won't; get off yourself," said I.

Before I knew what had happened two of the greasers grabbed me around the throat so I couldn't holler, and two others pulled off my coat, which they threw from the train. The fellow who had spoken to me told me that if I didn't jump off the train as soon as she slacked up they'd throw me off. I knew they would do so when opportunity offered, so off I hopped, mad as blazes. As I didn't want to lose my coat I walked back to get it and I had to walk a mile or so to do so. Luckily, I found my coat not far from the track and after putting it on, I faced eastward again toward the station. It is no joke to hike through an unfamiliar wilderness at night with no habitation or human being in sight or anyways near.

The night was a fine one, clear, cold and star-lit, so I managed to walk along the ties without serious mishap. In the sage brush, as I walked along, I could hear the sudden whirr of birds as they flew off startled, and the suddenness of the noise startled me at first for I didn't know what made the noise. But I quickly caught on.

In the distance I could hear the melancholy yelp of a coyote which was quickly answered from all points by other animals of the same species. One or two coyotes can make more noise than a pack of wolves or dogs. They are animals of the wolf species and are death to poultry, sheep, little pigs and small animals generally.

I got to the little town safe and sound but it must have been after midnight when I reached it, for there wasn't a soul to be seen in the streets and all was quiet. The town was Wadsworth.

I walked to the pump-house of the railroad, which was situated along the tracks and where I could hear the pump throbbing, and talked to the engineer, who didn't seem averse to a chat. His vigil was a lonely one, and anything to him was agreeable to vary the monotony. During the course of the conversation I learned that an eastbound freight would be along in a few hours.

I made the freight all right by riding the brakes. The train was made up of closed box-cars and there was no other way to ride except on the bumpers. I preferred the brakes.

It was pretty cold riding during the early morning hours, but luckily I had my overcoat with me once more, which helped to keep me warm.

Beating one's way is a picnic sometimes, but not always. During the summer time there is dust and heat to contend with, according to how one rides, and in winter time there are cold winds, snow and frost.

I rode the brakes all night and was glad when day broke. I was quite numbed.

The scenery was still the same—plains and alkali. At Lovelock I had time to get a bite of breakfast and a cup of hot coffee, and then the train was off for Humboldt. The distances between towns were great, about a hundred miles or so.

Finally the train stopped at Winnemucca, a town which, for short and sweet, is called "Winnemuck" by the knowing ones. At this place I concluded to hop off for a rest. Winnemucca is quite a sizeable town, and is the county seat of some county. It contains about two thousand inhabitants, and used to be as wild and woolly a place as any in the West, but it has tamed down some since. Saloons are plentiful and all drinks are ten cents straight, with no discount for quantity. A pretty good meal can be had for two bits, but short orders and such things as life preservers, sinkers, or a bit of "mystery" with coffee, are all the same price—two bits. I found no place where I could get anything for less.

There was a river or creek at the further end of town wherein I wished to bathe, but the water was so intolerably filthy that I deemed it wise to wait until I found a more suitable place along the route.

I noticed a bank in Winnemucca and was informed that it had been robbed recently of many thousands of dollars by bandits. Soon after the robbery a trellis-work of structural iron was put up from the money-counters clear to the ceiling with mere slots for the receiving and paying out of money, so that the next set of bandits who call there will have to crawl through mighty small holes to make a raise.

The next town along the line which amounted to anything was Elko and I made it that same day on a freight. I found it a pretty little town with good people in it, who treated me well. I learned there were some wonderful natural hot springs about a mile or so from town, so that afternoon I hiked out to see them. I shall never regret having seen them for they are one of nature's wonders.

Out in the wilderness, near where they were situated, I came upon an amphitheater of hills, at the base of which was a little lake about 100 yards in diameter. The hills were bare and lonely and near them was no house or habitation. All was wild, lone, still.

I climbed down one of these hills to the lake and had a good survey of it. The water was clear and pure as crystal but near the banks were sulphur springs which bubbled up now and then. The water was so hot it was impossible to put a finger in it.

I walked around the banks and at one end of the lake there was a hole so deep I couldn't see bottom. This is a crater-hole so deep that bottom has never been found, although it has been sounded to a depth of several thousand feet. The entire place looks like the crater of an extinct volcano. A single glance would lead anyone to suppose so.

Indian men, women, boys and girls go to the lake during the warm seasons to bathe, and many a daring buck who has swum across the crater was drowned in it and his body has never been recovered. I needed a bath myself so I disrobed and plunged in. The water was neither too hot nor too cold but half way between the two. It was just right. Where I swam was not in the crater but near it. The water there was part crater water and part sulphur water from the springs. The bath was delicious.

The ride eastward from Elko was uneventful. There was nothing to see but bare plains and mountains and a few border towns. The towns were very small, and hardly more than railroad stations. They were composed of a general store or two, several saloons, a blacksmith shop, drug store, bakery, butchershop, barber-shop, and that is all.

I boarded a freight train at Wells and rode the brakes through the Lucin Cutoff to Ogden. The trains used to run around Salt Lake, but now a trestle has been built through it, which saves many miles. The trestle is forty or fifty miles long, I should judge, and as I clung tightly to my perch on the brakebeam and looked down into the clear blue water through the ties I got kind of dizzy, but met with no disaster.

After a long and tedious ride of several hours I reached Ogden, the end of the S. P. line. As funds were low I remained in Ogden several days and went to work.

Ogden is in Utah and full of Mormons. It is a beautiful city, surrounded by lofty mountains, the Wasatch range, and contains about 50,000 people. It has a Mormon tabernacle, tithe-house, broad streets, fine stores, elegant public buildings and is quite a railroad center.

I happened to discover a Mormon lady who had a wood-pile in her back yard and she was needing a man to chop the wood, so we struck a bargain. I was to receive a dollar and a half per day and my board for my work and was given a room in an outhouse to bunk in. The terms suited me. The board was plentiful and good, and the sleeping quarters comfortable. I never saw a man about the place and wondered whether the lady was married or not. She was old enough to be. I knew she was a Mormon because she told me so, and possibly she was the plural wife of some rich old Mormon. I didn't like to ask too many questions for I might have got fired for being too nosy. The lady was sociable and kind-hearted and treated me well.

The Mormons like apples, cider and ladies, and they are an industrious people. The Bible says they can have all the wives they want, but the United States law says they can't have 'em, so what are the poor fellows to do? Sh! They have 'em on the sly. Don't give me away. Can you blame a rich old Mormon for having a big bunch of wives if he can support them? If I had the price I'd have two, at least, one for week days and one for Sundays, but if the mother-in-law is thrown in, I pass. One good healthy mother-in-law of the right sort can make it mighty interesting for a fellow, but a bunch of them; whew! Excuse me! During my stay in Ogden I didn't see any funny business going on, and wouldn't have suspected there was any, but from what I could learn on the outside, there was something doing. I saw lots of rosy-cheeked Mormon girls in the tabernacle one day when I was there, but they behaved just like other girls. The tabernacle is a church and it ain't. It is an immense egg-shaped building arranged very peculiarly, yet it is snug and cosy inside. It can hold thousands of people. It must be seen to be appreciated. I liked Ogden very much and would like to linger there longer but I deemed it best to keep a moving.

After leaving Ogden the scenery became interesting. The country is mountainous going eastward, and we struck a place called Weber Canyon, which is a narrow pass between high mountains through which the railroad winds. The mountains were pretty well wooded. In one spot I saw a place called the Devil's Slide, which was made by nature and consists of two long narrow ledges of rocks that begin high up on a mountain side and run down almost to the bottom of the mountain where the car tracks are. These rocks form two continuous lines that run down side by side with a space of several feet between them, and they are rough and raggedy on top. Imagine two rails with about four or five feet of space between them running down a mountain side several hundred feet and then you will have some idea of the formation of the slide. How in the devil the devil rode it, gets me. He must have been pretty broad in the beam, and I would like to have seen him when he performed the act. He must have come down a-flying, for the slide is nearly perpendicular.

This kind of scenery, though wild, was a relief from the bare and lonely plains of Nevada, and I appreciated it. A little variety is the spice of life, they say, and after seeing dullness it is nice to see beauty.

I was now on the Union Pacific Railroad and was in an empty cattle car, through the slats of which I could see the scenery on both sides of me. During the daytime it was nice, but at night the weather grew cold and the long watches of the night were dreary. A companion then would have been agreeable. I missed little Billy. At a small station in Wyoming called Rock Creek, I was put off the train one afternoon and as I hadn't a dime left, I felt it was incumbent on me to go to work. I saw a bunch of cattle in a corral near the railroad station that had probably been unloaded from a train, and as there were some bull-whackers with them I struck them for a job.

"Kin you ride?" asked a chap who looked like the boss.

"Ride anything with hair on," replied I.

"Ever herd cattle?" asked the boss.

"I'm an old hand at the business," answered I.

"Where'd you do your herding?"

"In California."

I never herded cattle in my life, but I could ride all right, and as I didn't consider bull-whacking much of a job, I thought I could hold it down easily. The boss hired me then and there at twenty dollars per month and chuck, and while on the range my bedroom was to be a large one—all Wyoming. It didn't take the cowboys long to get on to the fact that I was a tenderfoot, but as I was a good rider they said nothing. They were a whole-souled, rollicking, devil-may-care set of fellows, and the best they had was none too good for me. They treated me like a lord.

They knew, and the boss soon found out that I didn't know any more about roping a steer than a baby did, but as they were not branding cattle just then, that didn't matter so much. I got on to their way of herding quickly enough, and that was all that was necessary just then. I didn't ask where the outfit was bound for, nor did I care much, for all I was after was to earn a few dollars.

There were a good many hundred head of cattle in the bunch and many of the them were steers, but there were also many dried-up cows among them and some yearlings. They had all to be herded carefully so they wouldn't stray away, and to accomplish this we had to keep riding around them all day long. At night after feeding, the cattle rested. On dark nights they generally squatted down contentedly and chewed the cud, but on a moonlit night they would keep on their feet and feed. The very first moonlit night I was put on watch I got into trouble. The cattle arose to feed, and do what I would, I could not keep them together. When riding along on one side of the herd to keep them in, a few ignorant brutes on the other side would wander away and at such times some hard riding had to be done to keep them in. I could do it, but I couldn't ride everywhere at once.

I did some pretty fast riding and kept yelling and hallooing at the cattle, but one of the brutes got so far away from me that when he saw me coming he raised his tail and bolted outright. By the time I got him in others were scattered far and wide. I now saw that I was helpless, so I went to camp and aroused the sleeping cowboys. They knew instinctively what the trouble was and got out of their warm blankets cussing to beat the band. They mounted their ponies and off we all rode to gather the scattered herd. It was no picnic. There were four of us, and as the cattle had strayed off in all directions, it is easy to imagine what our task was. One of the boys and myself traveled together in one direction and made for an ornery brute that shook his head when we gently told him to "git in there." Off he shot like a rocket with a bellow of defiance, and his tail in the air.

"I'll fix the ugly son of—!" yelled my comrade, as he uncoiled his rope from his saddle and got it ready for a throw. His pony was after the steer like a shot, for it knew its business, and got in range in a jiffy. Out flew the rope and settled around the steer's neck. Quick as a flash the steer flew in the air, turned a complete somersault and landed on the turf with a jar that shook the earth.

"You will run away, you — —!" exclaimed the irate cowboy. "I guess you won't do it in a hurry again, gol darn your ugly hide."

The animal got up meek as a lamb, trembled in every limb, shook his head in a dazed way, and probably wondered what had struck him. We had no trouble with him after that, and made off after the rest. It was long after midnight before all the cattle were rounded up. The boss was mad clear through. The next day he politely told me that I didn't understand my business; that I didn't know any more about herding cattle than a kid; that I had lied to him about being a cowboy and that I had better skip. He cursed me up and down and kept up his abuse so long that I finally got tired of it and fired back. That made matters worse. We soon were at it, tooth and nail. He struck me with his fist and it was a hard blow. I was taller and longer in the reach than he and kept him off from me. The first blow was the only one he struck me, but it was a good one and dazed me for a moment. "I knowed you was a Greaser," yelled he as he danced around me, "and I'm going to put you out of business."

"Come on, you—," yelled I.

He wasn't in the mix-up at all. I was younger, stronger and longer in the reach than he, and one of the blows I put in was a tremendous one, for it knocked him down and he lay still for awhile. When he got up I knocked him down again. I saw he was my meat.

"Now, pay me off, you—, and I'll get out of here pretty darn quick; if you don't, I'll beat the life out of you," yelled I. The cowboys stood by and said nothing. It wasn't their funeral.

The boss paid me off and I got out.

At Cheyenne, Wyoming, I ran across a gassy little red-headed Hebrew who put me on to a good, money-making scheme. He had a lot of paste-board signs with him on which were neatly printed such things as: "Our trusting department is on the roof; take the elevator"; "Every time you take a drink things look different"; "In God we trust; all others must pay cash"; "We lead; others follow"; "Razors put in order good as new," etc., etc. The young fellow told me that he was beating his way to the Coast and that he sold enough of these signs to pay expenses. He told me also that the signs by the quantity cost him only five cents each, and that he sold them readily for twenty-five cents each.

I thought the little chap was lying for I didn't think anyone would pay twenty-five cents for such a sign, but he solemnly assured me on his word of honor that he had no trouble selling them at the price. He further told me that he would sell me a hundred of the signs at cost price, adding that if I bought a hundred of them, he would give me the address of the wholesaler in Omaha where I could obtain all the signs I wanted. The little scheme looked good to me but unfortunately I had only two dollars in my possession. This I offered him for forty signs with the name of the wholesaler thrown in. He accepted. I soon found that the little Israelite had told me the truth, for the signs sold readily for two bits each, though in some places I had to do a deal of talking to sell a sign, and in other places they laughed at me, when I told them the price was twenty-five cents, and offered me ten cents. As I wasn't sure whether I could purchase any more signs at the price I paid for them, I was loath to sell them for ten cents each.

When I reached Omaha I found the address of the sign man, and learned that I could buy all the signs I wanted in hundred lots at three cents each. The little cuss had done me after all.

I bought a hundred signs and now felt that I had struck a good thing, for I would have to do no more hard work. I sold many of the signs in small towns and cities, and found little difficulty in doing so. No more handouts for yours truly, no more wood-chopping, no more cow-punching. I was a full-fledged merchant and able to hold my own with any of them. It was easier sailing now.

The trip from Omaha to Chicago was interesting, but uneventful. At Omaha I crossed the muddy-looking Missouri River on a bridge while riding the bumpers of a freight, but was detected and put off on the other side of the river.

That night I did rather a daring thing. Along toward nine o'clock there came along a passenger train and as I had made up my mind to get on to Chicago as fast as I could, I stepped upon the platform of one of the passenger coaches and climbed upon the roof of the car, where I rode along for many a mile. Bye-and-bye, however, the wind became so keen, cold and cutting, and the rush of air so strong, that I became numbed and was obliged to climb down for warmth. I walked boldly into the passenger coach and sat down in a vacant seat near the door. I knew the conductor would not be round again for some time, for he had made his round, so for the present I felt safe.

When taking up tickets the conductor of a train usually starts at the front end and moves along to the rear. After his work is ended he will rarely sit down in any of the middle coaches, especially if every seat has an occupant, but he and the brakeman usually go to the smoker and sit down there. I was in the coach next to the smoker, and later on, I saw the conductor coming around again for tickets, I leisurely strolled to the rear platform of the car I was in and climbed on top again. I watched the conductor and waited until he had made his rounds, and then I returned to my seat in the coach.

In this way I traveled a long distance. I kept up these tactics for hours, but bye-and-bye I noticed a young woman who was traveling with her husband (a young fellow of about twenty-five), watch me suspiciously. She put her husband on to my little racket, and he, most likely, told the conductor, who laid a cute little trap to catch me. After he had been through all the coaches on his next round he went to the smoker, as usual, but when he came to the rear coach I was in he locked the rear door behind him. It was through this door I had been making my exit. He then passed slowly through the train again from the front looking at the hat checks. When I saw him coming and the brakeman following in the rear I tried the usual tactics but found the door locked. I was trapped. The conductor came up to me and seeing no hat-check asked me for my ticket. I pretended to look for it, but couldn't find it. The conductor eyed me coldly and told me to follow him to the baggage car. The brakeman acted as a rear guard. When we stepped into the baggage car the conductor asked me a few questions which to him did not seem satisfactory, whereupon he sternly warned me to get off at the next station. "If I catch you on here again, I'll throw you off," threatened he.

I knew he dared not legally throw me off a train while it was in motion, and that he was bluffing, but I got off at the next station just the same. I concluded I had ridden far enough that night, anyway. My journey to Chicago was soon completed.

I remained in Chicago several days selling the signs for a living but found it difficult work. The sign that seemed to sell best in Chicago was the one reading: "Every Time You Take a Drink, Things Look Different," and it made quite a hit in the saloons, but I could only get ten cents for it. The Chicago saloon keepers wanted all the money to come their way. In the smaller towns this sign sold readily for twenty-five cents, and no questions asked. I concluded to shake the dust of Chicago off my feet in a hurry, for the grafting was too hard for me. I had got onto it that there were easier places.

It was the Michigan Central that had the honor to yank me out of Chicago and a hard old road she was to beat. Spotters were everywhere—fly cops and bulls—and they gave me a run for my money. I gave some of them a cock-and-bull story about trying to get to a sick relative in New York City, and showed them the signs I was selling to help pay expenses. Some laughed, and told me to "git," but one or two sternly told me they had a mind to run me in. They didn't, though. I got along all right as far as Detroit, where I crossed over to Windsor, Canada, on a boat which ferried the whole train over at once. I was now in a foreign country, but everything there looked pretty much as it did in the United States. The Michigan Central took me clear through Canada to Niagara Falls, where I concluded to remain a few days, for much as I had heard of the Falls, I had never seen them.

I found that there is a big city of about 25,000 people at the Falls called "Niagara Falls," and it is a beautiful place.

On the Canadian side there is a little city, too, the name of which I forget. It is not nearly so large as the city on the American side, but it is a quaint and pretty little place.

Niagara Falls City is something like Coney Island, only it is on an all-the-year-round scale. Ordinary electric cars run through the place, electric tourist cars that will take one over the Gorge Route for a dollar are there, and so are hotels, boarding and rooming houses, plenty of stores, an extensive government reservation called Prospect Park, a Ferris Wheel, Shoot-the-Chutes, candy and ice cream booths, a hot frankfurter booth, picture galleries, beer gardens, etc. The place is lively and pretty, but full of grafters. Why wouldn't it be, when suckers by the million flock there every year from all over the world?

I got to like the place so well that I remained there nearly a week and learned a whole lot of things.

I wasn't a sucker and didn't get catched for I wasn't worth catching. Small fry ain't wanted. Did I see the Falls? Did I? Well, you can bet your sweet life I did. I saw them early, late and often, and every time I saw them they made my hair rise higher and higher. They are stupendous, tremendous—well, I can't say all I feel. They will awe anyone and fill him chock full of all kinds of thoughts. I'll try to give you an idea of them.

Niagara River is a stream about half a mile wide and about a hundred miles long. It connects Lake Erie with Lake Ontario, and as the waters of these great lakes form the river, the volume of its waters is great. About twenty-five miles from Buffalo the Niagara River enters rocky canyons, which are formed by Goat Island, and which divide the river. The rushing, roaring and leaping of the waters on either side of the island is tremendous. These rushing, roaring waters are called the Upper Rapids. The waters rush along at cannon-ball speed almost until they reach a hill about 165 feet in height. Down this they tumble. That constitutes the

Falls.

The river, as I said, is divided by Goat Island, so that one part of the stream shoots along the American shore and the other part along the Canadian.

By far the greater part of the river rushes along the Canadian side, hence the falls on that side are much greater than on the American. In fact, the American falls ain't a marker to the Canadian. I saw the falls from both sides, and when viewed from the Canadian side they are indescribably grand. No words of mine can describe them. You can hear the thunder of the rushing, roaring, falling waters a mile off, and the spray that arises from the depths below after the fallen waters have struck the rocks can be seen at a great distance.

While the great lakes flow and the Niagara River runs, this scene of rushing, roaring, tumbling waters will never cease. After the waters take their tumble they flow on placidly enough until they strike another narrow gorge or canyon, about a mile below the falls, which is called the Lower Rapids. In them may be seen a wicked whirlpool, the Devil's Hole, and other uncanny things.

Niagara is great, but the grafters who are there are greater. They will fool the stranger who goes there so slick that he won't know he has been fooled. The majority of visitors don't care, for they go there to spend their money, anyway. Some do care, however, for their means are limited. The grafters, who are not only hackmen, but storekeepers and others, lie awake nights studying how to "do" you. It is their business to make money, but how they make it don't worry them. If you go to the Falls, beware of them.

People from every nation under the sun flock to the Falls every year, as I said, and a million visitors a year is a low estimate, I am sure.

There are some people who believe that this great work of nature ought to be preserved intact, but there are others who do not think so. The latter think the Falls were created for their benefit, so they can make money. I am not now speaking of the grafters, but the manufacturers who have established factories along the banks of the Niagara River and utilize its waters for running their machinery, etc. These people would drain the river dry were they permitted to do so, and were doing so until stopped by the Government. I make no comments on this but simply state the facts and let others do the commenting.

After I had done the Falls pretty thoroughly I concluded to go to Buffalo, the beautiful city by the lake (Erie). It can be reached in several ways from Niagara Falls by trolley and by several lines of railroads. It cannot be reached by water, however, for the reason that the Upper Rapids in the river extend a mile or so from the Falls toward Buffalo, rendering navigation impracticable. The trolley line running from Buffalo to the Falls is one of the best patronized roads in the country, and is crowded every day and overcrowded on holidays and Sundays. The fare is fifty cents the round trip and the scenery, through which a part of the road passes, is very fine. The road runs pretty close to the Niagara River for quite a distance, and along the banks of the river may be seen manufacturing establishments, such as cyanide plants, paper mills, chemical works, etc., nearly all of which empty their refuse into the stream, polluting its waters considerably. All of these establishments can easily be seen near the river as you ride along in the trolley.

In the town of Niagara Falls itself are quite a number of very large manufacturing plants, which use the waters of the river for their purposes.

Buffalo is one of the handsomest cities in the United States, to my notion. Its water front along the business section of the town is pretty punky, for there is a vile-smelling canal in the vicinity, and malodorous streets and alleys, but otherwise the town is away up in G. She's a beaut, and no mistake. Delaware Avenue is a corker. Imagine a thoroughfare about 150 to 200 feet wide, with driveways in the center shaded by fine old trees, and ample sidewalks also shaded by fine trees. Along the sidewalks, but set far back, are roomy mansions that are set in ample gardens, and then you will have a faint idea of the beauty of Delaware Avenue. And there are many other streets in the vicinity of Delaware Avenue that are just as beautiful. Boulevards and fine streets abound in this fair city.

The people of Buffalo are quite like the Westerners in disposition, for they are sociable and free, and not too busy or too proud to talk to you. They are like their city, lovely, and I speak of them as I found them. There are many Canadians in the city (for Canada is only across the Niagara River and can be reached by ferry-boat) and I think they are a very desirable class of citizens. There are all sorts among them, of course, as is the case with Americans.

My signs went well in Buffalo, especially the one reading, "Every Time You Take a Drink, etc." It went well in the saloons along the water front and on Main Street, the leading thoroughfare. Lots of people laughed when they read it and said it was a good one. There is nothing like a laugh to put people in good humor.

I liked some of the Canadians very well and loved to listen to their queer accent. It is nothing like the American, but peculiarly their own. I thought some of the Canadian ladies were very nice.

I liked Buffalo so well that I concluded to remain there until I grew tired of it. After I had been there a day or so I became acquainted with a young girl whose front name was Rose. She was of an auburn type and very artless. She had a decided penchant for milk chocolates.

She was as pretty as a rose and it was awful hard for me to resist her. She was a poor, but good, honest, hardworking girl. She had been hurt in a street car collision and was just recovering from its effects. She craved chocolates but was too poor to buy them herself. I pitied her. She told me in her frank and artless way that she had thought a great deal of a certain young fellow, but he was in another city at present, working, and that she hadn't seen him for a long time. She didn't know whether she ever would see him again, but she hoped to, for he was a very sweet fellow, she said.

"If he thinks anything of me don't you think he'll come back to me?" she asked, turning up her soulful blue eyes at me.

"He would be a brute if he didn't, Rose," responded I, with considerable warmth. The girl surely loved him.

"Why don't he write to me?"

"Maybe he hasn't got the time or ain't much of a writer," said I. "Some people don't like to write."

"I guess that's true," said she, sadly.

Though she had a sneaking regard for the young fellow, she didn't object to me buying milk chocolates for her, nor to going to a show with me, nor to taking a ride to Crescent Beach on a cosy little lake steamer. In fact, Rosie was out for a good time, and evidently wasn't particular who furnished the funds. As I fancied the poor girl I was not averse to giving her a good time. We went to Delaware Park and spent several whole afternoons rowing on the little lake. We fed the ducks, walked in shady groves, and the time flew swiftly by in her company. During the morning I sold signs and in the afternoon I went with Rosie. I put in a whole lot of time in Buffalo with her, more than I should have done. One day I told her that I would have to go and then there was a kick. She wouldn't have it. She could not and she would not let me go, she said. I argued the case with her, but she wasn't open to argument. She was one of these kind of girls who are apt to forget the absent one when the present charmer is nigh. It was the hardest job in the world for me to leave her, but I finally did so. Rosie, farewell; and if forever, then forever, fare thee well.

CHAPTER IV.

NEW YORK CITY.

I have heard it stated that "a great city is a great solitude" and so it is if you are a stranger. New York seemed a big solitude to me, for I didn't know anyone and no one knew me. I landed in the Grand Central Depot in a swell quarter of the city one day, and felt utterly lost, for I didn't know which way to turn. As I was poor, that swell neighborhood was no place for me, but where was I to find a poorer locality? I concluded to walk and find one. I kept a walking and a walking and a walking, but the more I walked the more high-toned did the streets seem. Nothing but fine houses and well-paved streets met my view and they made me tired.

I did not like to address any of the people walking along these streets for they seemed hurried, cold and distant.

Says I to myself: "Windy, you've struck a cold place. Chicago was bad, but this place is worse. If you are going to Europe, this will have to be your headquarters for awhile, though."

Bye-and-bye I struck a street called Eighth Avenue, which was a long and wide one. It was full of people and stores. The sidewalks were so crowded that locomotion was difficult, and I saw more coons there than I had ever seen in my life before. They were dressed up to kill and considered they owned the town. From their manner one would suppose they had no use for white trash.

I had walked so much that I was pretty well tired out, and I also was hungry and thirsty. I concluded I would seek some saloon where I could obtain a rest, a drink and a free lunch, all for a nickel. There are such places everywhere in the cities, plenty of them, and all you have to do is to find them. I walked along and kept my eyes peeled for one. I saw lots of stylishly fitted-up stores along the avenue, and as there was so much style I thought there ought to be lots of money. Everyone I met was dressed to kill, and it seemed to me that no one was poor. Finally I came to a saloon which was bejeweled and be-cut-glassed outside, and swell inside, having marble floors and fancy fixtures. Into this saloon I stepped and strode up to the bar, where I ordered a schooner of beer. I laid down a nickel on the bar and then leisurely strolled over to the lunch counter, which contained a pretty good spread of free lunch. I tackled a fistful of bread and cheese, and then wound up with bologna, pickles, crackers and pickled tripe. I ordered another schooner and hit the free lunch again real hard. No one said anything to me. After a good long rest I hit the "Avenue" again to see the sights. There was plenty to be seen for the avenue was jammed with people, trolley cars and trucks. The buildings were of brick, as a rule, and old-fashioned in appearance. On the ground floor were stores and over head dwellings.

Everyone was a hustling and a bustling and didn't seem to have much time for anything except to sell you something. No one knew me or seemed to care a cuss for me. I felt lonely. The din was so great and the crowd so dense that I couldn't hear myself think. I was swept along with the crowd and kept my eyes and ears open. The stores were very fine, and the signs upon them handsome. Though Eighth Avenue is by no means in a rich section of the city, it seemed to me that there was a whole lot of wealth and style there. I felt quite out of place for I wasn't well dressed.

Some of the free lunch I had eaten—I believe it was the bologna—had given me a thirst, so I stepped into an ice cream saloon and had a "schooner" of ice cream soda, which quenched my thirst admirably. Things were cheap and good in New York, I quickly learned, and if one only had the price, one could live well there. One could have all kinds of fun, too, for there are so many people. The city is like an overgrown bee-hive—it more than swarms with people. I believe that New York City today has over four millions of people, with more a coming every year—thousands of them.

I had heard a great deal about the Bowery in New York, so I concluded to see it. I knew the song about it, the chorus of which was:

> The Bowery, the Bowery,
> They say such things, and they do such things,
> On the Bowery, the Bowery—
> Oh! I'll never go there any more.

And I was wondering what kind of things they said there and what they did.

Well, they didn't say much when I struck it and there was nothing doing to speak of, except people rushing along minding their own business. It may have been wicked, but it isn't now. It is a business street and that is all. There is an "Elevated" over the street, which makes noise enough to raise the dead, and a lot of cheap-looking stores and restaurants. There is any number of "hat-blocking" establishments run by Hebrews, and the whole street in fact, seems like a section of Jerusalem. Jews till you can't rest. There may be some knock-down-and-drag-out places, but these are not confined to the Bowery. There are other streets far worse.

No, the Bowery today is a peaceful, quiet street, and there isn't "anything doing" worth speaking about.

New York has some fine streets, such as Broadway, Fifth Avenue, Madison Square, Twenty-third Street, Fourteenth Street, etc. Broadway is the main business street and begins at Bowling Green and runs up to Central Park and thence beyond. It is several miles long, its lower portion from Bowling Green to Fourteenth Street being lined on either side by many sky-scrapers and massive wholesale business establishments, and from Fourteenth Street up, by retail stores. Rents are high on this street and the buildings fine. Fifth Avenue is not so long as Broadway and contains the residences of many millionaires and less rich people. There is lots of style and wealth on that street.

The Central Park is a beautiful spot. It runs from Fifty-ninth Street to One Hundred and Tenth Street, and from Fifth to Eighth Avenue. It is two and a half miles long by about two miles wide, and isn't big enough sometimes to contain the crowds of people that flock into it. It contains shady walks and trees, lawns, baseball grounds, lakes, casinos, stately malls (avenues), a large zoological collection, a great art gallery, an immense natural history building, extensive drives, secluded nooks for love-making, and lots of other nice things. Around its grand entrance at Fifth Avenue are some of the largest and swellest hotels in New York.

As everyone knows, of course, New York is the largest city in the country and the most cosmopolitan. It is the center of art, trade and finance, and its population is composed of all sorts. There are as many Irish as in the largest city in Ireland, as many Germans, almost, as in Hamburg, as many Jews as in Jerusalem, and a big crowd of almost every nationality under the sun. The main part of the city is situated on Manhattan Island, and it is overcrowded, compelling the overplus to seek the suburbs and other near-by localities. Even these are becoming too well populated. Jersey City, Newark, Brooklyn, Paterson, Kearney, Harrison, Staten Island, Coney Island, etc., are increasing in population all too rapidly. New York is one of the "step lively" towns, and you are expected to hustle there, whether you want to or not. It is all your life is worth sometimes to cross a street, and a car won't stop long enough to enable you to get on or off. The tenement sections are studies in human life, and malodorous ones at that. The throngs are wonderful to behold.

If you have plenty of money New York is an interesting place to live in. You will never feel dull there. You can live in some pretty suburb and go back and forth every morning and evening, as thousands do; or you can live in the city and ride out into the country every day by carriage, train or boat. In the good old summer time, if you live in the city, you can go to Manhattan or Brighton Beach, Coney Island, North Beach, South Beach, Rockaway, Fire Island, Long Branch, the Highlands, Shrewsbury River and a thousand and one other resorts in the vicinity. There is no lack of amusement or pleasure places.

Even the very poor can find lots of pleasant places to go, around New York, for the fares are low. For ten cents one can ride from New York to Coney Island, a distance of over twenty miles; to Fort George for five cents, fifteen miles or more; to Manhattan Beach, South Beach, Staten Island, Newark, up the Hudson, and lots of other places. In the city itself, and free for all, are the Aquarium, Art Galleries, Public Squares, Parks, Roof Gardens along the two rivers (the Hudson and East Rivers), the animals in Bronx and Central Parks, the museums and other things. There is always something to hear and see in New York City at all hours of the day and night.

New York surely is quite a sizeable village, and to judge from the way it has been growing, ten years from now it will extend a hundred miles or more up the Hudson, to Albany, maybe.

CHAPTER V.

THEM BLOOMIN' PUBLISHERS.

Before I say much more about New York I want to say a word about the book publishers of that city, for I got to know a little something about them. I will relate my experiences among them, which will enable others to judge what they are like. I wanted to find a publisher for this book, and was told that New York is the proper place to do business of that kind.

The first publisher I attempted to do business with has a large establishment on Vandewater Street, which is not far from the Brooklyn Bridge. I asked an elevator man who stood in the hallway of this building where I could find the boss.

"Which boss?" asked he, with a huge grin, for he probably deemed me some country jay looking for a job. My appearance was not very respect-inspiring, to say the truth; not for New York, anyway.

"The head of this establishment," answered I, placidly.

"What do you want to see him about? Are you looking for a job?"

"No, I'm not; I want to have some printing done."

"Oh, that's the ticket, is it? The superintendent is the man *you* want to see. He's on the top-floor. Come with me and I'll take you up to him."

I stepped into the elevator and up we shot. We never stopped until we struck the top landing, where a door confronted us which opened into a huge apartment that was full of type-stands, presses, paper-cutters and printing machinery of all sorts. At the furthest end of this huge apartment were some offices.

Upon my entrance into the large apartment a man stepped up to me and wanted to know what I wanted.

"I'd like to see the superintendent."

"Looking for a job, cully?" asked this gentleman.

"Well, hardly," responded I. "I want to have some printing done."

"Oh, you do, eh? You'll find the super in the rear office; away in the back," and he waved his hand toward the rear.

I walked toward the rear and was met by a small boy, who came out of an office and wanted to know my business.

"I want to see the superintendent, sonny," said I.

"What do you want to see him about?" asked the kid.

"Never you mind; I want to see him."

"Will you please let me have your card?"

"My card? What do you want my card for?"

"So as to let the boss know who you are."

"He don't know me; anyway, I haven't got a card."

"Will you please write your name and the nature of your business on this tab-let? and I'll take it to him," said the boy, handing me a writing tablet and pencil.

I didn't understand this method of doing business but I did as requested. The boy took the card in and presently the superintendent appeared. His name was Axtell.

"What can I do for you?" promptly asked Mr. Axtell, without any preliminar-ies. Probably he was a busy man.

"I have written a book, sir, and I want to have it printed."

The gent looked at me contemplatively. What his thoughts were I don't know.

"What kind of a book is it you've written? History, travel, poetry, novel or what?"

I told him it was a novel.

"How many pages will the book contain?" asked the superintendent.

"There will be four or five hundred pages, I guess, as near as I can figure it," responded I.

"How many copies will you want?"

"I'll leave that to you, sir, for you know best. This is my first book, and though I don't think it is going to set the world on fire," said I modestly, "I think a first edition of about ten thousand copies would be the thing. Don't you think that would do for a starter?"

"It might," said he contemplatively. "Excuse me," continued he as he sat down at his desk and began to do some figuring. When he got through he turned to me and said: "Ten thousand copies of the book in paper cover will cost you in the neighborhood of $1000."

"Cost *me* $1000," almost shrieked I. "I wanted to know what you'll give me for the manuscript and print it yourself."

A cold glare froze in the gent's eye. "We only print 'reprint' here; we do not buy manuscripts." I did not understand, and the gent judged so from my demean-or, for he added: "You want to see a publisher. Go up to Twenty-third Street; you'll find lots of them up that way."

I did not know the difference between a printer and a publisher at that time, so that is how I came to make the mistake.

Up Twenty-third Street way I went. Twenty-third Street was a pretty swell one, far too swell for rather a seedy-looking chap like me.

I came upon the establishment of Messrs. Graham & Sons, which was one of the swellest on the street. It was contained in a six-story marble building, all ornaments and furbelows in front, and it was so swell that it made me feel small. The store must have been at least 200 feet long and nearly as wide as it was long. A small part of this vast space was divided off into offices, but by far the greater portion was devoted to the exposure of books. Books were piled around till you couldn't rest—on counters, shelves, in elaborate glass cases, and on the floor, even. All were handsomely bound and good to look at. When I saw the conglomeration my heart sank.

"Look at all this array, Windy," said I to myself; "where are you going to get off at? You want to add another book to this little pile, do you? You are all kinds of a fool."

For a few moments I was discouraged, but the feeling did not last long. I am an optimist, a fellow who never gets discouraged. Instantly I mustered courage and walked up to a white-haired old gentleman whom I told that I would like to see the proprietor. The old gentleman told me that he was in his office on the top floor of the building. Up I went to see him. When I reached the top floor, which was a sort of literary symposium and printing office combined, a small boy came forward and asked me my business. I told him, whereupon he asked me for my card. As I hadn't any, I wrote my name and the nature of my business on a tablet, and the boy took it into an office. A well-groomed and handsome young gentleman came forward and asked me to be seated. It was in an outer, not walled-in office, but even the furniture in it was swell.

After exchanging airy compliments and discussing the weather a bit, the gentleman remarked *en passant*, "You have written a book?"

That broke the ice. I told him I had and then we proceeded to business. He wanted to know the nature of the book and such other things as were well for him to know. I then asked a few questions myself.

"What do you pay authors for their books, Mr. Graham?"

"That depends," replied he. "We usually pay a royalty of $500 down and ten per cent on every book sold, after that."

I thought that was a pretty fair rattle out of the box. I concluded to leave my writings with Mr. Graham on those terms and he consented to receive them. I knew he had but to read to accept. I always was optimistic, as I said before. Mr. Graham requested me to leave my address, so he could communicate with me. He informed me I would hear from him in a few days. I did. In a few days I got a note from him in a high-toned, crested envelope, which stated that "the first reader" of the house had read the book and found good points in it, but that "the second reader" was dubious. To make sure he, Mr. Graham, had read the book himself and wasn't certain whether there was any money in it. Under these circumstances he was constrained to forego the pleasure of publication, etc., etc., etc. These were not his exact words, but their substance. After reading the kind note I concluded to jump off the Brooklyn Bridge, but thought better of it. Messrs. Graham & Sons were not the only pebbles on the beach, so why not see what I could do elsewhere. That's what I did—tried my luck elsewhere. There were other publishers on Twenty-third Street and if Graham & Sons did not know a good thing when they saw it, others might.

On the same block, only a few doors distant, was another large firm. To them I went. A small little man with a Scotch accent sat in the ante-room and asked me what I was after. He wanted my card, too, but didn't get it. He went in to see Mr. Phillips, the editor of the publishing house, and this gentleman turned me down in short order. He told me that there are too many books published nowadays, and that books of travel were a drug on the market. The cuss told me everything in the world to discourage me, but he couldn't do it. I just went around to see some of the other publishers, but none of them would "touch" the story at any price and each one had a different reason for refusing. I was unknown, poor and obscure, and that settled it. There was no show there for me. To get along one must be rich or have "a pull."

CHAPTER VI.
THE OCEAN VOYAGE.

I put in the winter in New York working at Berry's, one of the swellest catering houses in the city. It is situated on Fifth Avenue and is a rival of the great Delmonico establishments. The nobs of New York, when they want to give a little dinner or supper at home, see Berry, who furnishes all the fine grub, cooks, waiters, dishes, plates, etc., or if they want to eat at his place they can do so, for he has private dining-rooms, ball-rooms, etc., where they can have anything they want, providing they have the price to pay for it. He employs a lot of people in his establishment, in the shape of a housekeeper, chambermaids, male chefs and assistants, waiters, omnibuses, porters, head-waiters, superintendents and a window-cleaner. I was the window-cleaner. It was the softest snap I had ever struck. I worked from 8 in the morning until about dusk, and all I had to do was to keep every window in the house as bright and shiny as a new dollar. The building is a large one and the windows are many, but it was no trick at all to keep them clean. I cleaned a few windows every day and put in a whole lot of unnecessary time at it.

I got twenty-five dollars a month for the job with board thrown in. The board was extra fine. Roast goose and chicken for dinner every day (left over victuals, of course), crab, shrimp and potato salads, oysters in any style, rich puddings, pies and cakes, wines of all vintages—say, sonny, we lived there and no mistake. I had struck a home. I held the job down all winter and saved a little money.

I told some of my fellow-workers, both male and female, that I intended to take a little flyer to the old country in the spring, and they laughed at me and guyed me unmercifully.

One fine spring day "when fancy lightly turns to thoughts of love" as I once saw it stated in a novel, I strolled down Bowling Green where the steamship offices are located and got pointers for my little trip. I learned that I could go to London direct, to Amsterdam, Rotterdam and several other dams; to Hamburg, Southampton, Liverpool, Havre, Glasgow and to so many other places that I grew bewildered.

As I stood in front of the Cunard line office a young fellow stepped up to me and asked:

"Say, mister, are you thinking of going to Yurrup?"

I didn't think it was any of his business, so I said:

"What do you want to know for?"

"Who, me?" replied he, taking time to gather his wits. "I'm connected with a ticket agency around on Greenwich Street, and if you want a ticket cheap, come with me and I'll get you one."

"How cheap?" asked I.

"That'll depend on where you want to go to. We sell tickets to all places mighty cheap. Where do you want to go?"

"Don't know yet; haven't decided."

"Let me sell you a ticket to Glasgow on the Anchor line. That line will take you to Ireland and Scotland and is the finest trip in the world."

"What's the fare?" inquired I.

"Only thirty dollars," answered he, "and you will get your money's worth."

I didn't think I'd see much of Ireland or Scotland if I bought a ticket from him, so I told him I'd see him later.

I wandered into the Anchor Line office and asked the ticket agent what the price of a ticket to Glasgow would be.

"Cabin or steerage?" inquired he.

"Steerage, of course; I'm no Vanderbilt."

The agent looked at me quizzingly and then remarked: "From twenty-seven dollars upward, according to accommodation."

I didn't know what he meant by "accommodation" but I thought twenty-seven dollars was enough for me.

"Do you want a ticket?" asked the agent, as if he were in a hurry.

"I haven't the price with me now," said I.

"What did you come here for then," snapped he.

"For information," snapped I.

He saw that I was getting huffy so he pulled in his horns and said: "We can take you to Scotland in pretty good shape for twenty-seven dollars. You will have a good berth and the best of food, and we'll land you in Glasgow in less than ten days from the time you leave here. What do you say; shall I give you a ticket?"

I cogitated. The prospect looked good to me.

"Yes," said I impulsively, "give me a ticket!"

I gave him my name, as he requested, answered all the questions he put to me, and in a jiffy he had the ticket made out for me.

"What's the name of the ship I'm going to sail on?" asked I.

"The Furnessia," answered he, adding, "she will leave from the foot of West Twenty-fourth Street on Saturday morning at nine o'clock sharp. Be on hand at that time, or you'll get left."

"Don't you worry about me getting left," retorted I; "I'll be there all right."

Was I happy after I bought the ticket? I can't say that I was, for I wasn't at all positive whether I had better go. I didn't know what the old country would be like, so that visions of all kinds of trouble floated through my noddle, but faint heart never won a fair lady. I might as well be found dead in Europe as in any other place. What's the dif?

This was Thursday and the ship was to sail on Saturday. It seemed to me a long time to wait for when I go anywhere I like to go in a hurry.

Saturday morning came and I arose bright and early. I slept very little that night, for I was thinking, thinking, thinking. After arising and having a cup of coffee I took my time strolling down toward the steamship pier. After I arrived there I was about to enter the long covered shed, when an official strode up to me and asked me where I was going. I carried no baggage of any sort and didn't think I needed any. I am too old a traveler to encumber myself with baggage. All I carried was on my person. I told the official I was bound for Europe on the Furnessia and showed him my ticket. He looked at it and let me pass. I went on board.

When I reached the deck a young man dressed in a white jacket and peaked cap asked me if I were a married man.

I didn't think it was any of his business, so I asked him what he wanted to know for.

The young fellow frowned and exclaimed: "Don't give me no language, young feller; I want to know if yer married or single." I told him I was a single man, whereupon he said: "You go forward to the quarters for single men!"

"Where's that?" queried I.

"For'ard of the main hatch," responded he. I didn't know the difference between a main hatch and a chicken hatch, but I went up to the front part of the vessel where I saw several sailors slinging trunks down a hole by means of a rope. I walked up to them and asked one of them who wasn't too busy to answer a question, where the main hatch was.

"It's in the fo'-castle," says Jack, with a wink at his mates; "do you want it?"

"No," said I. "I don't; where's the quarters for the single men."

"Oh, that's what you're after, is it? You follows your nose till you gets to the bows, and then you'll see a companionway down which you goes."

"All right," says I; "thank you." The directions weren't clear, but I guessed I could find my way. I went forward through rows of boxes, trunks, valises, ropes and other impediments, and finally came to a stairway over which was a hood or sliding cover. This stairway was almost straight up and down, with rough brass plates on each step to prevent one from slipping. At either side of it was a rope in lieu of a balustrade.

That stairway did not look good to me.

CHAPTER VII.

THE STEERAGE.

As soon as I tried to go down the stairway there was trouble, trouble of the worst kind. I could get down all right, but when I got down a few steps an odor came up that made me pause. The odor was not of stale onions, a rotting steer or anything like that, but an indefinable one. I never smelt anything like it before and it conquered me at once. It caught me right in the throat and though I tried to swallow I couldn't do so to save my life. I began to chew as if I were chewing tobacco, and the lump rose in my throat and wouldn't go up nor down. I hadn't drunk a drop that morning excepting a cup of coffee, so it couldn't have been liquor that upset me. It must have been the smell and nothing else. I stood on a step holding to the side rope to steady myself and hesitated about going down. I grew dizzy and thought I was going to fall but held on like grim death.

"Come Windy," says I to myself, "your bunk is below, and you'll have to go down to it or someone else will get it. This won't do."

I went down slowly and the further down I got the stronger the smell became. Suddenly I got very sick. I felt like giving up the enterprise right then and there but as my friends would have had the laugh on me if I did so, I concluded to see the thing out.

I had to go down the stairway, though, there was no getting around that; I had to select a berth, and to do that I had to go below. I kind of fooled around and hesitated to make the plunge but finally I mustered courage and made the attempt once more. I went down very slowly, holding my hand over my nose and mouth. I got down a few steps and then I stopped again. I just couldn't. I just laid down where I was and fired away like a good fellow. I was more than willing to die.

As I lay there a jacky suddenly came down, airy-fairy fashion, as if he were dancing on eggs, and in his hands he carried a long, black tin pan in which was his mate's breakfast, consisting of meat, gravy and potatoes.

I caught a whiff of the mess and oh mercy! When jacky got down to the bottom and saw me sitting there and the muss I had made he became very indignant and wanted to know what I meant by mussing up the ship like that.

"Why don't you go on deck if you want to be sick?" said he.

Had I been well I would have swiped the heartless cuss one just for luck, but I was too weak to speak, even. I fired away again and seeing this, Jacky flew away as if the devil was after him.

After a good long time I got down in the steerage and saw the steerage steward who was a Scotchman with a broad accent, and he gave me a berth. He noticed that I had been sick and advised me to go upstairs and get all the fresh air I could.

I acted on his advice and made my way up the stairway again as quickly as I could, but that wasn't very quick.

When I got on deck the fresh air revived me somewhat, but it seemed to me as if my stomach were all gone. There was an "all gone" feeling there, sure enough.

The ship was getting ready to start by this time. An officer mounted a raised deck over the forecastle and gave orders to heave the hawsers off. The captain, who stood on the bridge, signalled to the engineer below to let her go, and off we were.

Slowly we moved out from the pier, to the farewells of the multitudes on shore and on deck. Some blubbered, but ne'er a blubber from me. I wasn't caring whether school kept or not.

The vessel's prow after she got out of her dock was turned down the Hudson toward the Battery, and she went well out into the middle of the stream.

This afforded us a good view of the river. On one side was the New York shore, and on the other, the Jersey. Panoramas of houses and docks on either side swept by us as we moved along, and sky-scrapers loomed up prominently.

We passed pretty close to the Goddess of Liberty, and saw plainly Governor's Island, Ellis Island, Fort Hamilton, Fort Wordsworth, Bath Beach, Staten Island and Coney Island. Quickly enough we were abreast of Sandy Hook, which was the last point of land we would see until we reached Europe. Straight ahead of us was nothing but sky and water.

It was now nearly noon. I had eaten nothing that morning and what I had eaten yesterday was mostly downstairs in the hallway. The fresh sea-breeze had revived me a little and now I felt that I could eat something. None of the passengers had eaten anything since they came on board, and probably they, too, must have been hungry, for when the dinner bell rang there was a mighty stampede. Some of them didn't take time to rush downstairs, they just dropped down.

The dinner was good. There was plenty of nourishing soup on hand, a liberal allowance of meat, vegetables, bread, butter and coffee. No one need have gone hungry. All the other meals were satisfactory, though an occasional one was punky. Of course there were kickers, but those kind of people will be found everywhere.

The second day out was Sunday, and it was a fine spring day, but on Monday morning clouds began to gather and tried to work up a storm. They succeeded all too speedily. The sky became black, the wind roared up aloft, the masts hummed, timbers creaked, the ship rolled from side to side and then rose and fell; the cordage whipped against the masts and everything looked lovely for a first-class storm. I got scared. I hated to die so young, but what's the odds? The waves were high as mountains and to me seemed about as mean looking as anything I ever saw. They were white on top and made straight for us. We could not run away from them. I was on deck waiting to see the storm out, for what was the use going below and being drowned there? If I was to die I would die game and at the front. It didn't seem to me that anything built by human hands could withstand the buffeting of those waves. The force of the sky-scraping billows was awful. They kind of made me wilt when I looked at them.

I survived that storm or I wouldn't be writing this. If you catch me on the sea again though, you'll have to be a fast runner.

I was told that we would see land again by the following Sunday and I was sort of pining to see it. It was a wait of several long days, but I didn't have much else to do than wait. There was nothing to do on board except to eat, sleep and wait. I got pretty badly drenched during the storm. A huge comber made a leap for me and broke right over me, spilling a few tons of water on top of me. It was a soaker, sure enough, and I didn't dry out until several days afterward. I had only one suit of clothes with me and they were on my back so they had no chance to dry. I slept in them to keep them warm.

A life on the ocean wave is a gay thing. It is awful nice to be spun around like a cork and then see-sawed up and down with a possibility of touching bottom. The heel over from side to side is also very funny, for there is a good chance of being shot overboard when the ship jams suddenly away over. You hold on wondering whether the ship is going to right herself or not. If she does, you're in luck, and if she don't it's good-bye Lisa Jane. How many ships do tip over? Several thousand of them every year. Luckily, the Furnessia wasn't one of the unlucky ones this trip. The worst that happened to me was a bad scare and a shower-bath. Maybe the water wasn't cold when that wave struck me! Ugh! It knocked the wind out of me for a moment and I didn't know where I was at. I dripped like a drowned rat and when my fellow passengers saw me they roared.

On Tuesday morning of the second week we saw the shores of Europe. We had now been out about ten days. I have read that Columbus and his crew felt pretty good when they saw land again after their eventful voyage but I'll bet a dollar to a doughnut they didn't feel half as good as I felt when I saw land again. I was more than pining to see it. Ten days of sloppiness was a whole lot for me. If there is any fun wandering around with one's clothing sticking to one's back I fail to see it. I was feeling all right and my general health was good, but the lack of sleep and the fetid odors down below helped to daze me. I was in a sort of pipe dream and hardly knew whether I was afoot or on horseback.

There was land ahead, though, and I felt like shouting.

The land ahead of us was the coast of Ireland and it looked good to me. The name of Ireland was familiar to me since my boyhood days, and I had seen Irishmen on the stage and off it, had heard songs sung about it and had heard it spoken of a million times. Here was the real thing right before me. I became mightily interested in it as did almost everyone else. The Irish passengers aboard, and there were plenty of them, became frantic with joy. Ireland surely is a beautiful country. Rocky headlands we saw, capes, bays, towering mountains in the background, green trees and farms. An air of romance seemed to hang over the place and the blue skies of the spring above looked down on it kindly. We steered straight in for the shore and then sailed northward along the coast. We kept off shore only a few miles. When we got to Tory Island we steamed between it and the mainland, and had a close view of this little islet. It was only a mile or two long with a quaint looking light-house at one end of it and a vegetable garden in bloom near by. Those green things growing, how they did entrance me!

At the other end of the isle were rocks that towered up higher than the masts of our ship, and they were scarred, seamed and causewayed by the elements. They had taken the strangest shapes imaginable.

We steamed through the strait between the island and the mainland swiftly, for though the strait was narrow the channel was deep; then we skirted southward along the east coast of Ireland until we came to a broad bay, where we anchored. This bay was shallow close in to the shore, so we anchored far out. On the shore was the town of Moville, where the Irish passengers were to disembark for points in Ireland. A little tender came steaming up and when she was loaded with baggage and passengers, there was hardly room enough to swing a cat in but as the Irish passengers were happy, we had no kick coming. The warm-hearted Irish bade us farewell with many a thrown kiss and handkerchief flutter. They were off.

So we were soon, for Scotland. The scenes along the east coast of Ireland were no whit inferior to those on the west coast.

It did not take us long to reach Scotland, where the scenery was enchanting. Words are entirely inadequate to give one a proper idea of it. To be appreciated it must be seen and *felt*, for reading about it don't do much good.

Here, right before us, were the Highlands of Scotland and many a place famous in song and story.

In due course of time we reached the Firth of Clyde and anchored off Greenock. This was the disembarking point for all the passengers. A little steamer shot out from Greenock and landed us, bag and baggage, at the Princess Pier, which reminded me somewhat of a Mississippi levee, for it was stone paved and sloping. On the pier cabbies stood about, touching their hats respectfully, but saying never a word. They were seeking "fares," and giving us the tip noiselessly. Newsboys were there, too, yelling in strange accents, "Morning Nip!" "Daily Bladder," etc., and some of them when they got on to my presence and saw that I was a greenhorn, made loud uncomplimentary remarks about me in language that I couldn't understand. This rather embarrassed me, for I didn't like to be made a show of. Them kids ought to have got a kick in the pants for their freshness but the more you fool with some kids the worse they get, so I just walked on minding my business and said nothing.

All we third-raters were steered into the custom house where the baggage was to be examined. It didn't take the authorities long to examine mine. A quiet, lynx-eyed official asked me where my baggage was and when I told him I hadn't any, he jerked his head upward and backward, giving me a quiet hint to skip. I waited a few moments and then followed some of the other passengers to the railroad station, which was close by. Our destination was Glasgow, and Greenock was twenty-five miles distant, so we were compelled to make the rest of the journey by rail.

When I entered the railroad station I stood stock still for a moment and stared. On one side of the station was a blank wall and on the other a "buffet," waiting-room, ticket office, "luggage" room and telegraph office. What stumped me was the cars and locomotive. The cars were stage-coaches strung on wheels with no bumpers to speak of; no blind baggage, no brake-beams, no nothing. Where was a fellow to ride when he was beating his way? One couldn't beat it in any shape, form or manner. To say that I was disappointed won't express my feelings. I was totally discouraged. I felt like going back home again on the return trip of the Furnessia but I didn't have the price. I had less than fifteen dollars in my possession and was up against it. I had no idea how big a country Scotland was or how the walking would be, so I did some pretty lively thinking. I now remembered what Little Billy had told me and found out that he had told me the truth. No, there was no way of "beating it" on those kind of cars.

I mixed in with the push on the platform and began looking for a comfortable seat in a car. There were only two seats in a car, facing each other, and each seat was capable of holding four persons. Thus when there were eight persons in a coach it was full. I made a rush for a seat where I could view the scenery comfortably, and after the coaches were all filled and "all set," the doors were slammed shut, somebody outside blew a tin-horn and with a ratlike squeak from the engine we were off. The engine had seemed like a toy to me but she was speedy and powerful and could go like a streak. Away we clattered through tunnels, past fields and meadows, villages and towns. The scenery looked mighty foreign-looking to me and I was uneasy. I sure felt that I wasn't at home. On our right hand side as we sped up to Glasgow were the fields and meadows I just spoke of, and on the other side was a bare prairie through which wound the river Clyde. Along the banks of the Clyde were shipyards which are famous the world over. I believe these shipyards are so famous because ships can be built cheaper and better there than anywhere else. To be a Clyde-built ship is usually a recommendation. The scenery was interesting and would have been more so had I been happier. I was still half-dazed from the want of sleep during ten nights on board ship, my clothes didn't feel right on me from the soaking they had got and then the disappointment of not being able to "beat it," affected me, too. But it was all in the game, so I had no kick coming. After journeying about an hour we came upon the town of Paisley, which has been famous for centuries for the manufacture of "Paisley shawls." Large spool-cotton factories we could see in the place too, and it seemed to be a city of some size and consequence.

In a little while after that we rushed into St. Enoch's station, Glasgow. This was our jumping-off place. The station was a very large and fine one, almost as much so as the Grand Central Station in New York. To judge from the station, Glasgow must be a sizeable place, for it was first-class in every respect and right up to date.

CHAPTER VIII.

GLASGOW.

"All out for Glasgow," was the cry, so out we tumbled.

I made my way out of the station and soon found myself upon the street, where I stood perplexed and bewildered. It seemed to me I had landed in some other world. Everything was so different—the houses, the stores, the streets, the sidewalks, the driveways, the people, the vehicles, the dogs, the horses, the skies, the clouds, everything. How or where will I begin to describe these things? I have a pretty big contract on my hands, one that I am unequal to. I had never seen so many Scotch people in a bunch before and had no idea there were so many alive. There were thousands of them, tens of thousands of them. If Glasgow hasn't got a million of people then I miss my guess sadly. Scotchmen till you can't rest, anywhere and everywhere. Even the names on all the stores were Scotch. There was MacPherson and Blair, MacTevish, MacDonald, Brown, Alexander, MacFeely. Shetland ponies came trotting by that were about knee-high to a grasshopper and though so small they dragged after them carriages in which were seated grown persons. Why, a grown man could have picked up pony, rig and all, and carried them. I felt like telling the people in those rigs to get out and walk, and not disgrace themselves by making such a little creature in the shape of a horse drag them about. Oh, my! Oh, my! What queer things a fellow can see.

Here came a two-wheeled cart clattering along which was hauled by a melancholy-looking little donkey and it was called a "sweet-milk cart." I kept my eyes peeled to see if a "sour-milk" cart would come along, but I didn't see any.

They designate their stores in a curious way. A butcher shop is called a "flesher's," a furnishing goods store is called a "haberdashery," a dry goods store a "draper's," etc., etc.

Say, pardner, pinch me, will you? I wonder whether I am alive.

By this time I had stopped gazing standing still, and walked along, for the people were getting on to the fact that I was a greenhorn. My dress and appearance, and the way I stared gave me away. As I walked along unsteadily, still feeling that the ship was under me, I saw things. The houses were of gray stone several stories in height, with tall chimney tiles on top all in a cluster; stores on the ground floor and dwellings overhead. Nearly all of them had mansard roofs. They were nearly all alike and their exterior seemed plain and dull to me. But the stores riveted and held my attention. They were rather dingy, but the show windows were fitted up fine. Here was a fish store in the window of which were displayed salmon, grilse, lemons, plaice, megrins, haddock, cod, herrings; labels upon the platters designating what they were. In a candy store I saw toffie balls, chocolate bouncers, pomfret cakes, voice pastiles, and frosty nailrods. I laughed and wondered if they had any railroad spikes and rails. Frosty nailrods and bouncers, hey! Well, I was getting a pretty good show for my money. I looked into a tobacco store and there I saw a vast array of cigars, tobacco and smokers' articles. The brands of tobacco had curious names, such as Baillie Nicol Jarvey, Starboard Navy, Tam O'Shanter, Aromatic Mixture, English Birdseye and many others. The tobacco and cigars were dear, tobacco being eight cents an ounce, and funny-looking cigars four cents each. In the clothing store windows I noticed clothes made of excellent cloth in all varieties, that sold for eight and ten dollars the suit. They were fine and made me feel sad, for I hadn't the price to buy one, though I needed a suit badly. Shoes, too, were cheap and good. The windows of all the stores were heaped to profusion with goods, and it seemed to me there was more stock in the windows than there was in the stores. The wares were displayed very temptingly with a price tag on everything. The jewelry displayed was more than tasteful, I thought; I wanted a few diamonds awful bad.

I wandered along Argyle street, which seemed a broad and busy thoroughfare. The sidewalks were jammed and so was the roadway. I sauntered along slowly, taking in the circus, for it was better than a circus to me. It was a continuous performance. Lots of people gazed at me, nudged each other and made remarks, but I couldn't catch what they said. Probably they took me for some animal that had escaped from a menagerie. I wasn't caring, though, what they thought. I was having as much fun out of them as they were having out of me. I saw so many queer sights that I couldn't describe a tithe of them. Many fine people drove by in fine rigs, and some of these wealthy ones were probably out on shopping expeditions. There were grand ladies and gentlemen in multitudes, and I figured it out that wealth and nobility must be pretty prevalent in Scotland. Many of the ladies were beauties of the blond type and the gentlemen were well-dressed and elegant in appearance. They carried themselves nobly and proudly and seemed stern yet manly. The ladies surely were engaging and I noticed several of them alight from moving street cars gracefully. They didn't wait for the car to stop, but swung off, alighting in the right direction every time. Had they been American ladies it is more than likely they would have landed on top of their heads. The Glasgow ladies have mastered the trick, all right, and mastered it well, for you can't down them, nohow.

As I sauntered along slowly, two young girls came along with plaid shawls thrown over their shoulders and when they got near me one of the girls collapsed and fell on the sidewalk. None of the crowd stopped, whereat I wondered, but I stopped to see what the trouble was. If the girl wasn't as full as a goat you may smother me. She must have been imbibing too much hot Scotch. The girl was in her teens, and quite pretty, and so was her companion. I felt sorry that so young and pretty a girl would make a spectacle of herself, so I strode up and asked if I could be of any assistance. The fallen one glared at me and the one standing on her feet trying to help her companion stared at me. My American accent may have been too much for her for she made no reply. I remained standing there, where-upon the sober one got angry and turned on me with the remark: "Did yer never see ah lassie fou?"

From her indignant tones and manner I saw that she was huffy, so I made tracks in a hurry, for I wasn't looking for trouble.

After seeing as much as I wanted to of Argyle Street, I walked toward the embankment of the Clyde River, which I could see not far away, and had a look at the shipping. The ships were as curious to me as everything else I saw in Glasgow, for they were distinctly foreign-looking and odd. Glasgow seemed a great port, for there were ships of all nations there. The banks along the water front were high and walled up with stone, forming fine promenades. Quite a number of very fine bridges spanned the stream and they must have cost a lot of money. They were of stone, iron and wood, and were equal to structures of their kind anywhere. I noticed that the water was of a dark chocolate color, which means—mud. The stream isn't very broad, but it is deep. I was speaking of the vessels! Well, they took my time. I had read of low, black-hulled, rakish crafts in pirate stories and these looked like them. Wonder if they were pirates? I didn't go aboard any of them to investigate.

Along the water front street opposite the embankment were hotels, stores, lodging-houses, ship-outfitting establishments, taverns, inns, and all manner of places catering to seafaring men. All of them seemed curiosity shops to me. My little pen isn't able to describe them. What's the use of trying?

I came upon a spot called for short and sweet "The Broomielaw," which was a section of the water front given up to the landing of "up-country" steamboats, which came down the various lochs, rivers, bays, "the Minch," and other waters of northern Scotland, and it was more than interesting to observe the little steamers when they came in. They were laden with cattle and people from the Highlands and elsewhere, and with produce and merchandise. Many of the people were dressed in togs that I never saw outside of a comic opera show and when cattle were unloaded from these long, narrow piratical-looking craft I had more fun watching them than I ever had in my life before. The cattle were mostly black like the ships, and a whole lot of tail-twisting and Scotch language had to be used before they would take the hint and go ashore. They didn't like the looks of things and bucked. The sights of the city bewildered them, no doubt, for they were used to quieter scenes. The cowboys had on Tam O'Shanter caps and wore not describable togs. They punched the cattle, twisted their tails and shouted words that the cattle maybe could understand, but I couldn't. Highland Scotch was too high for my nut.

Excursion boats came to the Broomielaw and dumped their passengers on the landing from the Harris, Skye, Stormaway, Fladda, the Dutchman and all the other places so renowned in Scottish stories. After dumping one lot of passengers and freight they took another load back to the same places. Had I had the price I would have gone up country sure, for there are a whole lot of things to be seen up that way. But by this time it was nearing noon and I was getting hungry, so I concluded that a good, square meal would do me good. The Broomielaw and the other places weren't going to run away, and I would have plenty of opportunities of seeing them.

CHAPTER IX.

GETTING A SQUARE MEAL.

I drifted along Salt Market Street and then came upon a street which, for want of a better name, was called Sauchiehall Street, in the neighborhood of which I saw a restaurant called the "Workingman's Restaurant," on the side-wall of which was painted in large letters the following bill of fare:

Tea, 2 cents.
Coffee, 2 cents.
Porridge and milk, 2 cents.
Sandwiches, 2 and 4 cents.
Eggs, 2 cents.
Ham and eggs, 16 cents.
Broth, 2 cents.
Pea soup, 2 cents.
Potato soup, 2 cents.
Beefsteak pudding, 4 cents.
Sausage, 2 cents.
Collops, 4 and 6 cents.
Dessert puddings, 2 cents.
Fish suppers, 8 and 12 cents.
Tripe suppers, 8 and 12 cents.

The bill of fare and the prices looked good to me and I concluded that this would be my dining place.

In front of the restaurant were two large show windows in one of which was displayed all kinds of bakery goods, such as large flapjacks, big as elephant ears, labeled "scones." They looked like flapjacks to me, but were bigger and thicker, and could be had for two cents each. One of them was enough for a square meal. I wanted something better than that, though, just then. There were big biscuits in the window, too, cakes of various kinds, tarts, etc. In the other window were huge joints of beef and mutton, meat pies, hog-meat in various shapes and styles, and other dainties. My teeth began to water as I eyed the display and a drop trickled down my chin.

"Lemme see, now; what'll I tackle?" says I to myself.

Some of the hog meat looked good to me and so did the beef and mutton. I was willing to spend two bits or so for a good square meal. While I stood gazing and deliberating a young girl with a shawl around her shoulders came up to me and addressed me:

"Hoo air ye?" asked she.

I thought she had made a mistake and had taken me for someone she knew, so I asked her if she wasn't mistaken in the person. Either she did not understand pure English or else she did not want to, for she kept up the conversation. It didn't take me long to catch on to the fact that she was bent on making a mash. She didn't know me from Adam, nor I her. She was light haired and pretty, and had a slight, graceful figure, which was not well hidden by a shawl, which she kept opening and closing in front of her. I concluded that I was in for joy the first thing. To tell the real, honest truth, I wasn't hankering for fun just then, for I was too hungry, but of course it wouldn't do to be discourteous to a stranger, and a pretty one at that. To her inquiry how I was, I told her "Tiptop," which she didn't seem to understand. She did catch on to it, though, that I was a stranger.

"Where'd ye come from, the noo?"

"The noo, the noo," thinks I. "What does she mean by that?" I caught on suddenly. "Oh, I just landed this morning from New York."

"Ho, yer a Yankee, then?" says she.

"No, I'm not," answered I. "I'm a Westerner."

"Ooh eye, ooh eye," repeated she twice, as if she didn't understand.

"What air ye going to do in Glesgie?" asked she in clear, bell-like accents. She came up pretty close to me and now I could detect from her breath that she had been indulging in Scotch bug-juice. This displeased me. I gave her a hint that I had had no dinner and that I was pretty hungry, but it was evident that something stronger than a hint would be needed to cut me loose from her. She began to coax and then suddenly she called me a bully. That got me off. I told her in pretty plain language that she was a trifle fresh and that I hadn't said or done anything to warrant her in calling me names. She didn't understand what I said, but I guess she could tell from my manner that I was angry, so her soft eyes gazed down to the ground sadly. I excused myself, left her and went into the restaurant. The unexpected interview had agitated me somewhat, but I soon got over it.

The front part of the restaurant was a sort of store, where edibles were displayed on counters and which could be bought and carried away, or eaten on the premises, as one chose. The rest of the apartment was divided off into cabinets having sliding doors to them. In each cabinet was a rough wooden table with backless, wooden benches, close up to it, and on either side of it. The cabinet wasn't big enough to turn around in, but it served the purpose for which it was built.

A young waitress came to the cabinet I had chosen as my retreat and asked me what I would have. When she heard my foreign accent it was all she could do to keep from sniggering. I asked for pea soup for the first course. It was brought to me and it was nice. While eating it, the door slid back quietly, and who do you think entered it? Guess! I'll bet you never could guess. Why, it was no one else than the young girl who had addressed me outside the restaurant. She had probably watched from the outside and seen in which cabinet I had gone and there she was, large as life. Tell *me* Scotch girls aren't cute. For a moment I was so flabbergasted you could have knocked me down with a feather, but I soon recovered my equanimity.

The girl asked me if she might sit down beside me. What could I say? Of course, I said yes. I kept on eating my soup and cogitated. If this was the custom of the country I didn't like it. Where I came from strangers were not in the habit of inviting themselves to dinner. The lassie (that's what girls are called in Scotland) chinned away to me, but I didn't understand her, nor did I care to very much just then. After the pea soup had disappeared I asked the lassie if she was hungry and she gave me to understand that she was not. Probably she had only come in for a social chat.

The waitress soon came in again and sniffed scornfully when she saw my companion there. She probably took me for a naughty man. All this goes to show how a poor, innocent fellow can get into trouble when he isn't looking for it.

I next ordered some roast mutton, potatoes and bread and butter. To the waitress's inquiry what I would drink I said "Water." The lassie looked at me reproachfully. I divined that *she* wouldn't have ordered water. While I ate the lassie chinned and seemed to stick to me as faithfully as a Dutch uncle to a rich relative. I don't think that she was fully aware of what she was doing or saying.

After I had finished the second course, the waitress made her appearance again and wanted to know what further would be wanted. I told her, nothing, whereupon she began to gather up the dishes and her manner proclaimed that the cabinet might be wanted for the next customer. I took the hint and withdrew and the lassie followed me out. Outside of the restaurant the lassie gave me a gentle hint that she knew of a snug place where we could have "a little smile" together, but I wasn't drinking just then and told her so. I was leery of her, in fact. How did I know who she was or what her little game was. I didn't know the language of the country, the laws, the customs or anything, so I proposed to proceed carefully. I shook the lassie firmly but politely as soon as I could and went my way.

CHAPTER X.

GLASGOW GREEN (OR COMMON.)

I concluded to go down toward the Clyde again but had some difficulty finding my way, for the streets were tortuous and winding, though quaint and old-fashioned. I had seen pictures of such streets on the stage and in plays. After much walking I came upon a thoroughfare called Stockwell Street which led direct to the quays. I walked to the Albert Bridge and contemplated its strength and solidity, and then walked in the direction of a park which I saw not far distant. I was informed by someone whom I asked that this was the Glasgow Common, or Green. The park, I should judge, is about two miles long by about half a mile wide, and is almost destitute of trees or plants. It is, in fact, nothing more than a bare public playground fitted up with tennis courts, cricket grounds, apparatus for gymnastic exercises, swings, a music-stand, etc. It surely is an interesting spot. The walks are long and numerous, resting-places are plentiful and near the river is a building used by the Humane Society—a hospital, most likely. A little way in from the entrance is a fountain that is worth describing. The "Glesgie" people seem to have a grudge against it for some reason or other, but it is a nice and elaborate work of art for all that. It is a large structure with a broad basin and many other basins that diminish in diameter as they near the top. The top basin is quite small. Around the largest basin are groups of life-sized figures representing the various races of man, such as Africans, Asiatics, Europeans, Australians and Americans. The figures are exceedingly well done. On the topmost pinnacle of the fountain is a heroic image of Lord Nelson, the great English Admiral. I thought the whole work was a most elaborate and fine one.

Being tired, I sat down on a bench to rest. There were not very many people in the park just then and I had a good view of everything.

Clear over on the other side of the park there wasn't a single person to be seen except a couple that sat on a bench making love in strenuous fashion. It was a workingman and a lassie. Did you ever watch a calf when it sucks its mother, how it makes a grab for a teat, rest awhile, then make another grab? That is the way that man made love. Suddenly he would throw his arm around the girl's waist, press her to him, then let go and take a breathing spell. The lassie sat quiet taking it all in and saying never a word. In a few minutes the man would make another grab, take a fresh hold and then let go again. It was a queer way of making love, I thought. The couple wasn't bashful a bit and evidently didn't care who saw them. I thought to myself that I would have to find some lassie to give me a few lessons in the art of making love in Scotch fashion, for I wasn't on to the game at all.

After a good long rest I strolled through the city to see some more of it. It was quiet in the park just then and nothing doing.

I came upon the old Glasgow Cathedral which is by far the oldest structure in the city and the most thought of by Glasgowites, but I was not much impressed by it. It is a thousand years old or more, is great in extent, is surrounded by ample grounds and is made of stone. It contains flying buttresses and some other gim-crackery but the whole thing is rather plain, black and dull. Sir Walter Scott in one of his novels describes it faithfully, and if any one wants to know more about it I politely request them to look up Sir Walter Scott. I ain't equal to the task of describing architecture in detail and such things.

Not far from the Cathedral is the Necropolis, a very ancient burial ground right in the heart of the city, almost. It is as ancient as the Cathedral, maybe. It is a pretty spot and I went all through it. It is built around a hillside and is of considerable extent. Along the street level are walks bordered by trees, shrubs and flowers, and as you ascend the hillside you will see elaborate tombs, monuments, shady nooks and bosky bowers. On the highest portion of the rather steep and lofty hill a fine view of Glasgow may be had, and here lies buried, beneath a fine monument, John Knox, the Reformer. The Scotch think a heap about Mr. Knox, but as I don't know much about him I can't say much. He must have been a wonderful man and he surely lies buried in a grand spot. As a rule I don't like to wander about in boneyards, but as this one was so pretty I was impelled to do so.

Let me say a few words about Glasgow in a general way before I continue my story.

Glasgow is the commercial metropolis of Scotland. It contains about 800,000 people, and in most respects is a modern city. It is the center of art, finance and trade, and what New York is to the United States, Glasgow is to Scotland. There is much wealth, style and fashion there, the people are workers and full of business. Wholesale and retail establishments abound, ship-building yards are numerous, as are foundries and manufacturing shops of many kinds. Chief of all the great industries in Glasgow is the ship-building. The business of the port of Glasgow is great and the volume of the shipping immense. These few pointers will reveal to you that Glasgow is not a jay town by any means.

CHAPTER XI.

HUNTING FOR A FURNISHED ROOM.

As I said before, when I landed in Glasgow I had only a few dollars in my possession, therefore I deemed it wise to make them go as far as possible, for I didn't know what I was up against or how I would get along. The country was strange and new to me, I didn't know a soul this side the water, I knew nothing of the ways of the country or the people, and hadn't the faintest idea as yet how I was going to get through the country. That I could not beat my way I had already learned, and as I am not very partial to hiking it over long distances, I cogitated. But what was the use of thinking or worrying? Didn't I have some money in my inside pocket? Of course I had, and it was time enough to worry when I was broke. "Sufficient unto the day is the evil thereof," has always been my motto, and I had been on the turf long enough to know that there is always some way out of a scrape when one gets into it.

What was the next event on the program? I had dined and seen considerable of the city and it was "more better" that I go and look up a furnished room. I had to have some place to sleep and the cheapest and most comfortable way, I thought, was to rent a room in a private family. I have slept in lodging houses time without number but they are too public and sometimes too noisy. For a good, honest sleep give me a private dwelling. I knew that I was looking shabby but good clean money looks good to a whole lot of people.

I wandered through Buchanan and Argyle Streets, the Trongate and Gallowgate Street, but couldn't find a "To Let" sign anywhere. This kind of stumped me. I asked some one if there were no furnished rooms to let in Glasgow and he informed me that there were lots of them but that I would have to look in the upper stories of the houses for the signs. I did so but saw very few of them. I tackled the first place where I saw one. It was in a three-story building along the Trongate and the structure didn't look good to me. There was a narrow, stone-paved hallway leading through the building and at the rear of it was a cork-screw-like stairway that wound upward. The hallway was as dim and dark as a dungeon and made me feel funny. But I was there for a purpose so there was no use getting scared of bugaboos. Up the stairway I went, slowly and cautiously, keeping my eyes peeled for obstructions. I came to the first landing, where there was a single strongly made wooden door. I saw a knocker on the door and rapped at it rather faintly for admittance. An elderly woman came to the door and demanded to know what I wanted. I told her I was looking for a furnished room. From my accent she gathered that I was a foreigner for she asked at once:

"Yer a furriner, ain't ye?"

I can't describe the Scotch accent just right for it ain't my language, but I will try to set down what the lady said to me as well as I can.

"Yes, ma'am," said I; "I arrived from New York today."

"Yer a Yankee, I believe."

"No, ma'am," responded I, "I'm a Westerner."

This evidently puzzled the lady for she murmured "Ooh eye! ooh eye!" in the same tone somewhat as the boozy lassie at the Workingman's Restaurant had done.

"What will ye be doin' in Glasgie?" asked the lady.

I was stumped for a moment. I assured her I was going to look for a job.

"What's yer trade?"

"Oh, I work at anything," I answered.

"Ah, then yer jack of all trades and maister of none."

I assured the lady that was about the size of it and she then asked me how much I wanted to pay for a room. I told her about a dollar a week. As things were cheaper on this side of the water than on the other side, I figured it out that I ought to get things at about half price. Evidently the lady didn't think so, for she scanned me scornfully and wanted to know if I took her place for a tramp's lodging house. That was putting it rather plain which caused me to kind of wilt. I assured the landlady I had no such idea. I asked her what she charged for a room and she said two dollars and a half per week. Too much for yours truly, I thought, and told her so. We couldn't make a deal so I groped my way down stairs and tried my luck elsewhere. Rents probably were high in that part of the city so I crossed the Clyde and wandered into the Gorbals district. This is a section of the city inhabited by the poorer classes of working people and I had my eye on it while wandering along the Broomielaw. I saw warehouses along the waterfront over there and stone-paved streets full of houses. The houses were ancient-looking and grimy but I would probably find what I sought there.

The first house I entered in that district had the same kind of a hallway with a spiral stairway at the end of it as the house I had been in on the other side of the river, and when I rapped at the door on the first floor a lady answered the summons. When I told her that I wanted a furnished room she wanted to know how much I was willing to pay. She did not tell me her price but wanted to size up my pile. Her little racket wouldn't work. I told her that if she had a room that suited me and if the price was right we could make a deal, otherwise not. Whereupon she opened her hall door, let me in and led me to a fair-sized room and asked me how I liked it. It contained a table, sofa and two chairs, but nothing else. I told her I wanted a bed-room, not a sitting-room.

"This is a bed-room," said she, opening a closet in the room in which was a bunk.

Holy Jerusalem! What did the lady take me for; a Chinaman, to put me in a china closet? Nay, nay, Pauline! I'm no Chinaman. Here was another case where the deal fell through. I like plenty of fresh air and light where I sleep when I can get it, and enough room to kick in. Here there was none of these things.

I kept a-moving. I came to a house opposite a theater where I met two young ladies who occupied a flat and had a spare room. I believe they were actresses. They told me that their vacant room was rented by an actor who was now making a tour of the cities and that they didn't know just when he would be home. In the meanwhile I could occupy his room if I wished and when the actor returned I could share the room with him. I did not feel as if I would like to sleep with an actor, for he might have been a snorer or a high kicker, and I didn't know when he would be back anyway. That sort of an arrangement did not suit me. No deal was made here, either.

The next place I went to and where I finally located, was a flat occupied by an old man and his daughter. The father was over seventy years of age and the daughter about thirty. They rented me a neat room for one dollar a week which contained an ample bed, chairs, rocker, a wash-stand, soap, towel, a window, lace curtains and a shade. My patience and perseverance had been rewarded at last. As soon as my landlady left me I stripped and took a wash from head to foot, the first good clean-up I had since I left New York. It was great. I rented the room for a week and concluded to hike out of town when the week was up. During the week that I remained in this house I became quite well acquainted with the old man and his daughter and learned that he was from the north of Ireland and that his wife who was dead had been Scotch. The daughter, therefore, was half-and-half. She was an amiable, good-tempered young woman, though far from pretty, and the devotion she showed to her father astonished me. He wasn't in the best of health and often was crabbed and cross, but no matter how crusty he was the daughter petted and humored him, and crowed and goo-ed and gaa-ed to him and never got out of patience. She treated him as a mother does her child and never wearied of soothing him. The old man didn't seem to appreciate these attentions for his daughter got no thanks from him and not even a kind word. One day when the daughter had gone out on an errand the father suspected that she was in my room, so he rushed into my room, looked under the bed and into the corners to see if she were there. The old man had not the slightest reason or cause to suspect his daughter and I watched his maneuvers with anger but said nothing. He deserved a good tongue-lashing and I felt like giving it to him but his great age held me back. Had he been a younger man I would have told him what I thought of him in short order.

CHAPTER XII.

DANCING IN THE GREEN.

I slept well that night, better than I had slept since I left New York, for there was nothing to disturb me. A good rub down and a good night's rest had done me a world of good. Those who have traveled know what my feelings were. After a cheap breakfast in a Municipal Restaurant, where I had two big, thick slices of bread with excellent butter and a cup of good coffee for two cents, I bummed around the Clyde again, taking in the sights. I liked Glasgow first rate. The people were as friendly and sociable as they were out West, and their accent and ways were a never-ending source of interest to me. Everything that I saw interested me, for it was all so new and strange. No one can have the faintest idea what there is to be seen abroad unless he or she goes there and hears and sees for himself. Word-pictures are inadequate to give one a proper idea, for there is something even in a foreign *atmosphere* that must be felt before it can be appreciated.

I bought a morning paper and sat down on a bench along the embankment to read it. It was interesting from start to finish with nothing "yellow" about it. The articles were written in an able, scholarly way, and besides giving the news there were columns devoted to giving useful hints, such as "Master and Man," "Husbands and Wives," and such like things, that were well to know. They were in the shape of "Answers and Queries," somewhat. Even the advertisements were interesting to me but "The Want" ads were mostly incomprehensible, for there were too many Scotch colloquialisms in them. I saw an announcement in the paper stating that there would be dancing in the Green that afternoon, and I concluded instantly that I would take it in. It was to be a free show and when there is anything of that sort going on you may count me in, every time.

In the meanwhile I just loafed around the banks of the Clyde, watching them load and unload vessels, taking in the foreigners' ways of doing things, peering into the shop-windows along the water-front, etc. The time passed quickly enough. I wasn't homesick a bit but felt right at home. There was something about the people and the place that made me feel quite at home.

After dinner, at about two o'clock, I strolled into the Green. People were slowly sauntering into it in groups, and walking up toward the music stand where the dancing was to be done. The music stand was about half a mile from the park entrance. It was early, so I sat down on a bench and made myself comfortable. Little boys came along handing out programs and I secured one of them. Here is what it said:

Glasgow Green.

No. 1—March; Glendaurel Highlanders.

No. 2—Strathspey; Marquis of Huntley.

No. 3—Reel; The Auld Wife Ayont the Fire.

No. 4—March; Brian Boru.

No. 5—Strathspey; Sandy King.

No. 6—Reel; Abercairney Highlanders.

No. 7—Dance; Reel o' Tullock.

No. 8—Waltz; The Pride of Scotland.

No. 9—Highland Fling.

No. 10—March; Loch Katrine Highlanders.

No. 11—Strathspey; When You Go to the Hill.

No. 12—Reel; Over the Isles to America.

No. 13—Dance; Sword Dance.

No. 14—March; 93d's Farewell to Edinburgh.

No. 15—Strathspey; Kessock Ferry.

No. 16—Reel; Mrs. McLeod's.

No. 17—Slow March; Lord Leven.

Choir.

No. 1—Glee; Hail, Smiling Morn.

No. 2—Part Song; Rhine Raft Song.

No. 3—Part Song; Maggie Lauder.

No. 4—Part Song; Let the Hills Resound.

No. 5—Scottish Medley, introducing favorite airs.

No. 6—We'll Hae Nane But Hielan Bonnets Here.

No. 7—Part Song; Hail to the Chief.

No. 8—Part Song; The Auld Man.

No. 9—Part Song; Awake Aeolian Lyre.

No. 10—Part Song; Night, Lovely Night.

No. 11—God Save the King.

The program was a good long one and sure looked good to me. I imagined there would be something doing.

At about half past two there was a big crowd congregated about the music stand but as there were few seats near it most of the people had to stand.

As I wanted to see all I could I mingled with the throng and patiently waited for the performance to begin. The band hadn't made its appearance yet and there was no one on the band stand. To relieve the tedium some of the young fellows who were in the crowd began to chaff some of the lassies in a flirty way. Three pretty girls in a group were the especial target of the laddies. If I could only get off the Scotch right I would jot down some of their badinage for it was very amusing, to me, at least, but I couldn't do the theme justice.

After what to me seemed an interminable long wait we heard some yelling and snarling away down toward the entrance of the park I took to be dog-fighting. Too bad it was so far away, for anything would have been agreeable just then to relieve the monotony, even a dog-fight. I noticed the people near the entrance scattering to either side of the walk and forming a lane through which to give the dogs a show. The yelping and snarling came nearer and finally I perceived that it was a band of men approaching dressed in Highland costume and playing the bagpipes. I had heard the bagpipes played many a time and knew what they were but I had never heard a whole lot of them played at once. I now knew that it wasn't a dog-fight that had caused the noise. The bag-pipers came along quickly with long strides, their heads erect, stern of visage with petticoats flying from side to side like those of a canteen-girl when she marches with her regiment. The men were husky fellows, broad-shouldered, lithe and active, but they wore no pants. The whole lot of them were bare-legged and upon their heads was perched a little plaid cap with a feather in it, and over their shoulders was thrown a plaid shawl. Stockings came up to their knees, but their legs a little way further up beyond the stockings were entirely bare. Although there were lots of the girls present I didn't notice any of them blush at this exposure of the person. Maybe they were used to such spectacles. What tune do you think these Highlanders were playing as they marched along? Nothing more nor less than—

> "Where, oh where has my little dog gone,
> Where, oh where can he be?
> With his hair cut short and his tail cut long,
> Where, oh where can he be?"

This was a mighty nice little tune and I had heard it before, but I had never heard it played by such instruments. The people liked the tune and seemed to like the Highlanders too, for when they went by, the people closed in after them in a solid body, and marched behind them, a pushing, elbowing, struggling mass.

When the music stand was reached the band did not go upon it but marched around it playing that same little old tune. I wondered why they didn't change it and play something else but as the crowd didn't kick there was no use of me kicking. They kept a marching and a marching around the stand for quite a little while but the tune never changed. The musicians took a good fresh hold on the air every minute or two, some note rising a little shriller than the others but that is all the variation there was. Do you want to know the honest truth? Well I wasn't stuck on the tune or the bagpipes either. The noise they made would have made a dog howl. It was nothing but a shrieking, yelling, and squeaking. Call that music? From the pleased faces of the people you would have judged it was fine.

After what seemed a coon's age the band quit playing and marching, and mounted the platform, upon which they had been preceded by a lot of boys and girls who formed the choir.

Number one on the program was a march, the Glendaurel Highlanders. I couldn't see anything in it except more marching to a different tune. The crowd seemed to like it and applauded frantically. There was a whole lot of pushing and shoving by the crowd in my neighborhood and I wasn't comfortable at all. A sturdy dame behind me made herself especially obnoxious by wanting to get right up front and she didn't seem to care how she got there or who she shoved out of the way to accomplish her purpose.

She dug her elbow into my side in no gentle fashion, and was bent on getting in front of me, whether I was agreeable or not. Well, she didn't make the riffle. I planted my elbow in her rib to see how she liked it. She scuttled away from me then quickly enough.

Number two on the program was Marquis of Huntley. I didn't know who the Marquis of Huntley was but evidently the crowd did for they went wild over the tune and dancing. The dancing was fine, tip-top, but I can't say as much for the tune. The way them Highlanders could dance was a caution, for they were graceful and supple as eels. No flies on them.

Number three was a corker, a reel called "The Auld Wife Ayont the Fire." There was something doing this time. The Highlanders turned themselves loose and they hopped, skipped, jumped and yelled like a tribe of Sioux Indians on the war path. How they did carry on and how the crowd whooped it up in sympathy! The whole push was frantic, Highlanders and all. My hair riz but I don't know why. If any one tells me that those bare-legged Highlanders can't dance I will surely tell them they are mistaken. They were artists and no mistake, every one of them.

Brian Boru was the next event on the program, a march. I was getting tired of marches but the mob wasn't. They applauded the Brian Boru wildly and saw a whole lot in it that I couldn't see.

Number five was another strathspey, Sandy King. I was wondering who Sandy was and if he were a king, but I didn't like to ask questions. No use letting the "hoi-polloi" get on to it that I was a greenhorn. There might have been something doing had they known it, for it takes but a little thing to set a mob a-going.

Next came a reel, Abercairney Highlanders. I wondered how many different clans of Highlanders there were in Scotland. The woods seemed full of them. This was another wild Indian affair, worse than the first reel. Them chaps were good yellers and jumpers, and I think could hold their own with any wild Indian, no matter what tribe he belonged to. Their lungs were leathery, their limbs tireless, and their wind excellent.

The Reel of Tullock came next and then a waltz, "The Pride of Scotland." Both were excellent.

Number nine was a Highland Fling. That was a great number. It aroused everyone to enthusiasm. I could not help but admire the grace of the dancers. So quick they were, so unerring. Their wind was so good that I felt I would have hated to tackle any one of them in a scrap.

Number thirteen was a sword-dance, danced by one man only. Crossed swords were laid on the platform and the highlander danced between them slowly, rapidly, any old way, and never touched. He never looked down while dancing, and how he managed to avoid these swords was a marvel to me. The sword blades were placed close together and the dance was kept up a long time. That chap was an artist of a high class, and could have made a whole lot of money on the stage had he chosen to do so. Maybe he was a celebrity in Glasgow and Scotland. He never touched a sword. His dancing was marvelous. It was evident these Highlanders could do something besides squeezing wind out of a bag and playing "where, oh where." Yes, they were all right. Their performance was a good one and worth anyone's while to see. When I returned to my lodgings that evening I told my landlady that I had attended the dance in the Green and she wanted to know how I liked it. I told her truly that it was the best I had ever seen. And it was, by long odds.

CHAPTER XIII.

TAKING IN A GLASGOW SHOW.

The evening of my second day's stay in Glasgow I put in by taking in a show at the theater. It was the Gayety Theater I intended to go to, where vaudeville plays were given, but as the theater was a long distance from the Gorbals District, I had some trouble finding it. The theatrical performances in Glasgow begin early, some at half-past five and some at six o'clock, and let out at about nine o'clock, which gives those so inclined a chance to go to bed early. The days were long at that season of the year, so that I arrived in front of the theater while the evening sun was still high in the heavens. The theater building was an immense one of stone and very lofty. In front of it was a long line of people waiting to make a rush for good seats in the gallery, and I joined the throng. There was a good deal of rough horse-play among some of the fellows waiting there and a whole lot of chaffing. A chap behind me gave me a kick in the rump and tipped my hat over my eyes, which he deemed a very good joke. I didn't think it was and told him not to get too gay, whereupon he roared with laughter. He told his neighbors that they had a greenhorn among them, whereupon many in the crowd made life a burden for me for a while. They made all kinds of chaffing remarks, they jeered me, they hooted me and groaned. They were having a whole lot of fun at my expense but I never said another word, for what was the use? I was mad clear through, though. Had I only had a gang with me there might have been a different tale to tell. I was alone and friendless. A fellow thinks all kinds of things when a crowd gets after him.

The line was growing longer rapidly, and before the doors were opened a couple of hundred people must have been on the street waiting. As soon as the doors were opened there was a grand rush and scramble to secure tickets. I held my own in the push, though I was nearly suffocated and squeezed flat, but managed to secure a ticket after a little while, for which I paid twelve cents—six pence. Cheap enough if the show is any good. I rushed up the spiral stairway after the crowd, but before I got half way up I was obliged to stop and blow off steam. The steps were many and winding. I did not notice anyone else stopping for a breather which led me to conclude that the Scots are a long-winded race. Two or three times did I have to stop before I reached nigger-heaven, my destination. The gallery was so high up and so close to the ceiling that I could have touched the ceiling with my hand when standing up. Below, clear to the orchestra seats, or "pit," as it is called, was gallery after gallery. Some of these were divided off into queer contrivances called "stalls." To me the stalls seemed like huge dry-goods boxes, with the part facing outward, toward the stage, open, from the middle to the top. The lower part was boarded in. They were queer-looking contrivances, and the people in them looked as if they were caged. The stalls were supposed to be private and exclusive—in a word, private boxes.

Some little boys in livery were wandering about on the various floors crying out "Program" with the accent on the first syllable, and as I wanted one, I hailed a boy who gave me one and charged me a penny for it (two cents). Printing must be dear in Glasgow, I thought, to charge a fellow two cents for a printed piece of paper. I said nothing but scanned the program. Here is what it said:

No. 1—La Puits d'Amour, Balfe; Band.

No. 2—Mr. John Robertson, Baritone Vocalist.

No. 3—Drew and Richards in their specialty act, Old Fashioned Times.

No. 4—Mr. Billy Ford, Negro Comedian.

No. 5—The Alaskas—Ben and Frank—Comic Horizontal Bar Experts.

No. 6—Mr. Edward Harris, London Comedian.

No. 7—Miss Josie Trimmer, Child Actress, and the Forget-me-nots, Vocalists and Dancers.

No. 8—Selection, Yeoman of the Guard.

No. 9—Sallie Adams, American Serpentine Dancer.

No. 10—The Gees, in their Musical Oddity, Invention.

No. 11—Collins and Dickens, in their Refined Specialty act.

No. 12—Mr. Charles Russell, Comedian and descriptive Vocalist.

No. 13—National Anthem.

Quite a lengthy program this and it looked to me as if it might be good, especially the Serpentine Dancer, who was a countrywoman of mine, and the darkies, who were probably countrymen.

After a moderate wait the lights were turned up, the orchestra tuned up and soon the band gave us a selection by Balfe called "La Puits d'Amour." I didn't know what "La Puits d'Amour" was but it didn't make any difference to me. It was some kind of music. The selection was a long one and the band sawed away at it as if they were never going to stop. It was so long drawn out in fact that my wits went a wool gathering and I nearly fell asleep, for tedious music is apt to make me snooze. When the music stopped I woke up and was ready for business.

The first event on the program was Mr. John Robertson, Baritone Vocalist.

The band played a preliminary flourish when out walked Mr. Robertson dressed in a spike-tail coat, black vest and biled shirt. Hanging in front of his vest was a long, thick watch-chain which must have been a valuable one, for it looked like gold. Mr. Robertson sang a song and kept a hold on his watch chain. The song was hum-drum and so was Mr. Robertson's voice. Mr. Robertson made no great hit and when he left us he took his chain with him.

Number two was Drew and Richards in their specialty act, "Old Fashioned Times."

A lady and gent came upon the stage dressed in very old-fashioned garb, and sang. Just as soon as the lady opened her mouth to sing I knew she was a gentleman and she couldn't sing any more like a lady than I could. I have seen female impersonators on the stage many a time and they carried out the illusion perfectly, but this chap wasn't in it at all. He gave me a pain. I wasn't sorry when this couple made their exit.

Mr. Billy Ford, the Negro Comedian, next came to the front. Now there'll be a little something doing, anyway, thought I.

Mr. Billy Ford was not a negro at all but a Britisher with a cockney accent. Maybe I wasn't astonished! Holy Smoke! He sang out bold as you please just as if he were singing like a darkey and the gallery gods went into ecstacies over him. They laughed, roared, and chirruped. They seemed to think a heap of Mr. Ford, but I felt like going somewhere to lay off and die. A nigger with a cockney accent! Oh my! Oh my! Will wonders never cease?

The comic horizontal bar experts, the Alaskas, were very tame turners, and to my view, anything but funny. I had seen better stunts than they performed in free shows on the Bowery at Coney Island.

The sixth number on the program was Mr. Edward Harris, London Comedian. Here at last was someone who could sing and act. Mr. Harris was from the London Music Halls and was evidently a favorite, for he was given a great reception. He was greeted with roars of welcome and shouts and calls from the gallery gods that seemed unfamiliar and queer to me. Even the people in the pit and stalls applauded loudly. Mr. Harris turned himself loose and impersonated London characters in a way that brought forth the wildest enthusiasm. Some of the gods nearly died laughing at his comicalities and a man away down in the pit laughed out loud in such a way that it made me think of a dream I once had when I saw ghosts playing leap-frog over a graveyard fence and having an elegant time of it. The noise this man made was a high sepulchral shriek, like theirs. It was wild and weird.

The comedian was first class and the audience was loath to let him go. They recalled him several times and he responded.

Number seven was Miss Josie Trimmer, child actress, and the two Forget-Me-Nots, vocalists and dancers. This was another tame affair for the two Forget-Me-Nots were Scottish lassies who got off coon songs with a Scotch accent and had acquired an improper idea of coon dancing. Their act was a caricature and a— well, never mind. It isn't right to be too critical. They were doing the best they could and were appreciated by the audience, so it may be well for me not to say too much.

The next number was a selection by the band, "Yeoman of the Guard," which was played after a long intermission. I was getting rather weary by this time and had half a mind to go home, but I wanted to see the serpentine dancer, Sallie

Adams, who was a countrywoman of mine. It seemed to me I hadn't seen a countryman or countrywoman for a coon's age, and I felt as if I just couldn't go until I saw Sallie.

When the time came for Miss Adams to appear on the stage, all the lights in the theater were turned out and a strong calcium light was thrown upon the stage. Sallie hopped into view chipper as you please, never caring a whoop who saw her, countryman or foreigner, and she began to throw diaphanous folds of cheese-cloth all over herself and around herself. Different colored lights were thrown upon her draperies as she danced, and the effect was thrilling and made my hair stand up. Sallie was all right. She was onto her job in good shape. Maybe I didn't applaud? I roared, I stamped and whistled, and my neighbors must have thought I was clean off. The gorgeous spectacle reminded me of the Fourth of July at home, when sky-rockets go up with a hiss and a roar, Roman candles color the black skies, sissers chase through the air like snakes, bombs explode and fall in stars of all colors. Siss! Boom! Ah!

When Sallie made her exit I made mine, for I had got my money's worth and was satisfied.

CHAPTER XIV.

MR. ROBERT BURNS, THE POET.

One thing that struck me very forcibly before I had been in Glasgow any length of time was the fact that the people thought a great deal of Mr. Burns, the poet. Streets and lanes were named after him, inns and taverns, shoes, hats, caps, clothing, tobacco, bum-looking cigars, bad whiskey, in fact his name was attached to all kinds of articles to make them sell, and in some cases merely as a mark of respect or affection.

It was plain to the most casual observer that Mr. Burns was thought a great deal of. He had been dead a hundred years or more, yet his personality pervaded the place, and his picture was to be seen on signs, posters, in the stores and elsewhere. For Mr. Burns most Scotchmen will die, Scotch ladies sigh, Scotch babies cry, Scotch dogs ki-yi. He was a good-looking chap, and highly gifted, but the poor fellow died before he had reached his thirty-eighth year, which was a national calamity. Had he lived there is no telling what he might have accomplished, for during the short span of his life he did wonderful things. He took the old Scotch songs that had been written before his day and gave them a twist of his own which improved them vastly, and made them immortal; he portrayed Scottish life in a way that no poet has ever imitated or will imitate maybe, and he loved his country deeply and fervently. His father was a rancher, and a poverty-stricken one at that, and the poet was born in a shack on the farm. The house was a little old one of stone, and a rich man of the day would have used it for a chicken house. In this house and in a china closet in the kitchen was born the greatest poet Scotland ever produced. When Bobbie grew up the old man set him a-plowing, and while at this work the boy composed rhymes which were so good that some of his friends induced him to print them. Old man Burns didn't see any good in the verses, for he knew more about poultry than he did about poetry, and told his son to cut it out. Bobbie couldn't, for it just came natural.

Before he was twenty-one the boy had written lots of good poetry and it was put in book form and printed at Kilmarnock, a town not far from his birthplace. The birthplace of the poet was on the farm near the town of Ayr, in Ayrshire, and that whole county (or shire) is now called "The Burns Country," because it was the poet's stamping-ground. The poet knew lots of people throughout the county and his writings have immortalized many a place in it. After his book had been printed he sprang into fame at once and was made much of by man, woman and child. Being a good-looking chap, the girls began to run after him, and poor Burnsie had the time of his life. He wanted to steer clear of 'em, but he couldn't, for the girls liked and admired him too much. The result was that a few of them got into trouble, and soon some wild-eyed fathers and brothers went gunning for him. The fault was not the poet's wholly, for he couldn't have kept these girls away from him with a cannon. To avoid such troubles in the future he finally married a blond, buxom young lassie called Jean Armour, by whom he had twins, the first rattle out of the box. Not long after that he had two at a throw again. Bobbie could do something besides write poetry, evidently. He was a thoroughbred any way you took him, though the people at that time did not know it and did not fully appreciate his great qualities. It was only after he had been dead a long time that the world fully realized his worth. At the present day they estimate him properly and their affection and reverence for him are boundless. Some of his countrymen call him simply Burns, others call him Rabbie, and still others, "puir Rabbie," puir meaning poor.

The country that he lived in, Ayrshire, is visited by a million strangers or more every year, who visit the shack he was born in and the places he made immortal by his writings. The shack has been fixed up and improved somewhat since he lived in it, and is now a sort of museum where are displayed various editions of the books, manuscripts and other things, that once were his. Among the things is a walking-cane that a New York lawyer named Kennedy somehow got hold of. How Kennedy got the cane I don't know, but he returned it to the Burns collection in the cottage. Mr. Kennedy is a rare exception to New York lawyers in general, for they rarely return anything that they once get their hands on. Mr. Kennedy must have had a whole lot of regard for the great poet.

Lots of people have never read any of Burns' poems. I wonder would they appreciate it if I showed them a few samples? I will not print the long ones, but only the shorter ones, for even they will show, I am sure, the greatness of "Puir Rabbie."

As I said in a previous chapter, when I first set foot in Scotland it was at Greenock, about 25 miles from Glasgow, where a tender took us ashore from the Furnessia. Greenock is quite a city, for it contains a good many factories and other establishments, but the city has become famous the world over just because of one little circumstance connected with the great poet, namely: A young girl named Highland Mary lived there who loved, and was beloved by the poet, and they were engaged to be married. Sad to relate, the young girl died while she was engaged to the poet, which saddened him considerably. Years afterward he married Jean Armour. The poet wrote some lines to the memory of Highland Mary which almost any Scotchman or Scotch lady can recite by heart. Here they are:

HIGHLAND MARY.

Ye banks and braes and streams around
The Castle o' Montgomery,
Green be your woods, and fair your flowers,
Your waters never drumlie;
There Summer first unfauld her robes,
And there the langest tarry;
For there I took the last farewell

> O' my sweet Highland Mary.
>
> How sweetly bloomed the gay green birk
> How rich the hawthorn's blossom!
> As, underneath their fragrant shade
> I clasped her to my bosom!
> The golden hours, on angels' wings
> Flew o'er me and my dearie;
> For dear to me as light and life
> Was my sweet Highland Mary.
>
> Wi' mony a vow and locked embrace
> Our parting was fu' tender;
> And pledging oft to meet again
> We tore oursels asunder;
> But, O! fell Death's untimely frost,
> That nipt my flower sae early!
> Now green's the sod and cauld's the clay
> That wraps my Highland Mary.
>
> O pale, pale now those rosy lips
> I oft ha'e kissed sae fondly!
> And closed for aye the sparkling glance,
> That dwelt on me sae kindly!
> And mouldering now in silent dust
> That heart that lo'ed me dearly!
> But still within my bosom's core
> Shall live my Highland Mary.

Was there anything ever written more sad, pathetic and sweet?

Following is a little poem written in a different vein which may serve as a sort of temperance lesson to some husbands who stay out late at night having a good time. The recreant husband's name in the poem is Mr. Jo, and Mrs. Jo sends it in to him good and hard. Says Mr. Jo:

> O let me in this ae night,
> This ae, ae, ae night;
> For pity's sake this ae night,
> O rise and let me in, Jo!
>
> Thou hear'st the winter wind and weet;
> Nae star blinks thro' the driving sleet.
> Tak' pity on my weary feet,
> And shield me frae the rain, Jo.
>
> The bitter blast that 'round me blaws
> Unheeded howls, unheeded fa's;
> The cauldness o' thine heart's the cause
> Of a' my grief and pain, Jo.
>
> O let me in this ae, ae night,

> This ae, ae, ae night;
> For pity's sake this ae night
> O rise and let me in, Jo.

Mr. Jo's pleadings were in vain, to judge from Mrs. Jo's answer, which is as follows:

> O tell na me o' wind and rain!
> Upbraid na me wi' cauld disdain!
> Gae back the gate ye came again—
> I winna let you in, Jo.

I haven't the least idea where Jo spent the night, but it surely wasn't with Mrs. Jo. There are lots of husbands who get full and don't know when to go home. Let them paste this poem in their hats. It may do them good.

Here is an old song revised by Puir Rabbie, whose magic touch has made it better and more famous than it ever was before. It is entitled: "Will ye go to the Highlands, Leezie Lindsay?"

> Will ye go to the Hielands, Leezie Lindsay,
> Will ye go to the Hielands wi' me?
> Will ye go to the Hielands, Leezie Lindsay,
> My pride and my darling to be?

> To gang to the Hielands wi' you, sir,
> I dinna ken how that may be;
> For I ken na the land that ye live in,
> Nor ken I the lad I'm gaun wi'.

> O Leezie, lass, ye maun ken little,
> If sae that ye dinna ken me;
> My name is Lord Ronald McDonald,
> A chieftain o' high degree.

> She has kilted her coats o' green satin,
> She has kilted them up to the knee;
> And she's off wi' Lord Ronald McDonald
> His bride and his darling to be.

A whole lot of human nature about this little poem and a fine swing to it. Burns had a touch that no one has ever imitated or ever can imitate. It is a twist, which for want of a better name, I would call "a French Twist." Imitate it, ye who can!

Everyone knows "Auld Lang Syne." It is an old song that didn't amount to much until Burns got a hold of it and put his twist to it. Here it is:

AULD LANG SYNE.

> Should auld acquaintance be forgot,
> And never brought to min'?
> Should auld acquaintance be forgot

And days o' auld lang syne?
For auld lang syne, my dear,
For auld lang syne,

Well tak' a cup o' kindness yet
For auld lang syne.
We twa ha'e run about the braes
And pu'd the gowans fine;
But we've wandered many a weary foot
Sin' auld lang syne;
We two ha'e paid'lt i' the burn
Frae mornin' sun till dine;
But seas between us braid ha'e roar'd
Sin auld lang syne.

Chorus.

And here's a hand, my trusty fren,
And gie us a hand o' thine;
And we'll take a right good wallie-waught
For auld lang syne.

Chorus.

And surely ye'll be your pint stoup,
And surely I'll be mine;
And we'll take a cup o' kindness yet
For auld lang syne.

Following is a composition that is famous the world over and is used as a recitation, not only in this country but in every other English-speaking country. It is entitled: "Bruce at Bannockburn":

BRUCE AT BANNOCKBURN.

Scots, wha ha'e wi' Wallace bled;
Scots, whom Bruce has often led;
Welcome to your gory bed,
Or to glorious victorie!

Now's the day, and now's the hour;
See the front o' battle lower;
See approach proud Edward's power —
Edward! chains and slaverie!

Wha will be a traitor knave?
Wha can fill a coward's grave?
Wha sae base as be a slave?
Traitor! Coward! turn and flee.

Wha for Scotland's king and law
Freedom's sword will strongly draw,
Freemen stand or freemen fa',

Caledonian! on wi' me!

By oppression's woes and pains!
By your sons in servile chains!
We will drain our dearest veins,
But they shall—they shall be free!

Lay the proud usurper low!
Tyrants fall in every foe!
Liberty's in every blow!
Forward! Let us do or die.

Here is a love song to Jennie, entitled, "Come, Let Me Take Thee!"

COME, LET ME TAKE THEE.

Come, let me take thee to my breast
And pledge we ne'er shall sunder;
And I shall spurn as vilest dust
The world's wealth and grandeur;
And do I hear my Jennie own
That equal transports move her?
I ask for dearest life alone
That I may live to love her.

Thus in my arms, wi' a' thy charms,
I clasp my countless treasure;
I'll seek nae mair o' heaven to share
Than sic a moment's pleasure;
And by thy een sae bonnie blue
I swear I'm thine forever!
And on thy lips I seal my vow,
And break it I shall never.

One day Burns was called upon for a toast during a dinner which was given by the Dumfries Volunteers, in honor of their anniversary. The poet got up and spoke the following lines extempore:

Instead of a song, boys, I'll give you a toast—
Here is the memory of those on the 12th that we lost!
That we lost, did I say; nay, by heaven, that we found;
For their fame it shall last while the world goes around.
The next in succession I'll give you—the King!
Whoe'er would betray him, on high may he swing!
And here's the grand fabric, our Free Constitution,
As built on the base of the great Revolution.
And longer with politics not to be crammed,
Be anarchy cursed and be tyranny damned;
And who would to Liberty e'er be disloyal,
May his son be a hangman and he his first trial.

A GRACE BEFORE MEAT.

Some ha'e meat and canna eat it,
And some wad eat that want it;
But we ha'e meat and we can eat,
And sae the Lord be thankit.

TO A HEN-PECKED COUNTRY SQUIRE.

As father Adam first was fooled,
A case that's still too common,
Here lies a man a woman ruled—
The devil ruled the woman.

The poet's father, William Burness, lies buried in a graveyard at Alloway. The following lines were written by his son to his memory:

LINES TO HIS FATHER.

O ye whose cheek the tear of pity stains,
Draw near with pious reverence and attend.

Here lie the loving husband's dear remains,
The tender father and the generous friend.

The pitying heart that felt for human woe;
The dauntless heart that feared no human pride;

The friend of man, to vice alone a foe;
"For e'en his failings leaned to virtue's side."

I believe there are some husbands who grow tired of the married state after they have been in it a while. They came to find out that it isn't all "beer and skittles," as they first imagined it would be. Even "Puir Rabbie" had troubles of his own, as the following will show, for it is written about himself:

"Oh, that I had n'er been married!
I would never had nae care;
Now I've gotten wife and bairns,
And they cry crowdie ev'ry mair;

Ance crowdie, twice crowdie,
Three times crowdie in a day;
Gin ye crowdie ony mair,
Ye'll crowdie a' my meal away.

Waefu' want and hunger fley me,
Glowrin' by the hallan en';
Sair I fecht them at the door,
But aye I'm eerie the come ben."

The poet had lots of cronies and friends, and he was as loyal to some of them as they were to him. He was a good boon companion and liked "a wee drappie" (nip) himself as well as anyone. Many an alehouse proudly proclaims that he visited it and preserves the chair or bench that he sat on, the glass he drank out of or the table he sat at, to this day, and any and every thing that is familiar with his presence is sacred and treasured. William Muir of Tarbolton is the friend to whom the following lines were written:

ON A FRIEND.

An honest man here lies at rest,
As e'er God with his image blest;
The friend of man, the friend of truth;
The friend of age, the guide of youth;
Few hearts like his with virtue warmed,
Few heads with knowledge so informed;
If there's another world, he lives in bliss;
If there is none he made the best of this.

Mr. John Dove kept an inn at Mauchline called the "Whiteford Arms," and the poet pays his respects to him in the following fashion:

ON JOHN DOVE, INNKEEPER.

Here lies Johnny Pidgeon;
What was his religion?
Whae'er desires to ken,
To some other warl'
Maun follow the carl,
For here Johnny Pidgeon had nane.

Strong ale was ablution—
Small beer persecution—
A dram was momento mori;
But a full flowing bowl
Was the saving his soul,
And port was celestial glory.

To judge from the following, the poet did not have a great respect for all ruling elders of the church. Souter Hood was a miserly one.

TO A CELEBRATED RULING ELDER.

Here Souter Hood in death doth sleep;
To hell, if he's gone thither;
Satan, gie him thy gear to keep,
He'll hand it weel thegither.

TO ANOTHER HEN-PECKED HUSBAND.

O Death, hadst thou but spared his life
Whom we this day lament,
We freely wad exchanged the wife
An' a' been weel content.

The poet was hospitably entertained at a place one day called for short and sweet Dahna Cardoch. In appreciation he got off the following:

> When death's dark stream I ferry o'er,
> A time that surely shall come—
> In heaven itself I'll ask no more
> Than just a Highland Welcome.

One Sunday while in the northern part of Scotland with Nicol, a friend of his, he visited the Carron Works which they had traveled some distance to see. There was a sign on the gate: "No Admittance to Strangers," which barred the poet and his friend. Here is an apostrophe by Burns in regard to the matter:

NO ADMITTANCE TO STRANGERS.

> We cam' na here to view your warks
> In hopes to be mair wise,
> But only, lest we gang to hell,
> It may be nae surprise;
> But when we tirled at your door,
> Your porter dought na hear us;
> Sae may, should we to hell's yetts come,
> Your billy Satan serve us.

LORD GREGORY.

> O, mirk, mirk is this midnight hour,
> And loud the tempest roar;
> A waeful wanderer seeks thy tower—
> Lord Gregory, ope the door.
>
> An exile frae her father's ha',
> And a' for loving thee;
> At least some pity on me show,
> If love it may na be.
>
> Lord Gregory, mind'st thou not the grove
> By bonnie Irwine side,
> Where first I owned that virgin love
> I lang, lang had denied!
>
> How often didst thou pledge and vow
> Thou wad for aye be mine;
> And my fond heart, itself sae true,
> It ne'er mistrusted thine.
>
> Hard is thy heart, Lord Gregory,
> And flinty is thy breast—
> Thou dart of heaven that flashed by,
> O, wilt thou give me rest!
>
> Ye mustering thunders from above,

Your willing victim see!
But spare and pardon my fause love
His wrangs to Heaven and me!

MARY MORISON.

O, Mary, at thy window be,
It is the wished, the trysted hour!
Those smiles and glances let me see
That makes the miser's treasure poor.
How blithely wad I bide the stoure
A weary slave frae sun to sun,
Could I the rich reward secure—
The lovely Mary Morison.

Jestreen, when to the trembling string
The dance gaed through the lighted ha',
To thee my fancy took its wing—
I sat, but neither heard nor saw;
Though this was fair, and that was braw,
And you the toast of a' the town,
I sighed and said amang them a'
"Ye are na Mary Morison."

O Mary, canst thou wreck his peace,
Wha for thy sake wad gladly die;
Or canst thou break that heart of his
Whose only faut is loving thee?
If love for love thou wilt na gi'e
At least be pity to me shown,
A thought ungentle canna be
The thought o' Mary Morison.

TO A LAIRD.

When — — deceased to the devil went down
'Twas nothing would serve him but Satan's own crown;
Thy fool's head, quoth Satan, that crown shall wear never,
Grant thou'rt wicked but not quite so clever.

OPEN THE DOOR TO ME, O!

O, open the door some pity to show,
O, open the door to me, O!
Though thou has been fause, I'll ever prove true,

O, open the door to me, O!
Cauld is the blast upon my pale cheek,
But caulder thy love for me, O!
The frost that freezes the life at my heart

Is naught to my pains frae thee, O!
The wan moon is setting behind the white wave,
And time is setting with me, O!
False friends, false love, farewell! for mair
I'll ne'er trouble them nor thee, O!
She has opened the door, she has opened it wide;

She sees his pale corse on the plain, O!
My true love! she cried, and sank down by his side
Never to rise again, O!

TO CARDONESS.

Bless the Redeemer, Cardoness,
With grateful lifted eyes;
Who said that not the soul alone
But body, too, must rise.

For had he said, "The soul alone
From death I shall deliver,"
Alas! alas! O Cardoness,
Then thou hadst slept forever.

YOUNG JESSIE.

True hearted was he, the said swain o' the Yarrow,
And fair are the maids on the banks o' the Ayr,
But by the sweet side of the Nith's winding river
Are lovers as faithful and maidens as fair;
To equal young Jessie seek Scotland all over,
To equal young Jessie you seek it in vain;
Grace, beauty and elegance fetter her lover,
And maidenly modesty fixes the chain.
O, fresh is the rose in the gay dewy morning,
And sweet is the lily at evening close;
But in the fair presence o' lovely young Jessie
Unseen is the lily, unheeded the rose.
Love sits in her smile, a wizard ensnaring,
Enthroned in her een, he delivers his law;
And still to her charms she alone is a stranger,
Her modest demeanor's the jewel of a'.

DOWN THE BURN, DAVIE.

As down the burn they took their way
And thro' the flowery dale,
His cheek to hers he aft did lay,
And love was aye the tale.
"O, Mary, when shall we return

Sic pleasure to renew?"
Quoth Mary, "Love, I like the burn,
And aye shall follow you."

A BIT OF ADVICE.

Deluded swain, the pleasure
The fickle Fair can give thee
Is but a fairy treasure—
Thy hopes will soon deceive thee.
The billows on the ocean,
The breezes idly roaming,
The clouds' uncertain motion—
They are bu t types of women.
O! art thou not ashamed
To doat upon a feature?
If man thou wouldst be named,
Despise the silly creature.
Go, find an honest fellow—
Good claret set before thee—
Hold on till thou'rt mellow—
And then to bed in glory.

MY SPOUSE NANCY.

Husband, husband, cease your strife,
No longer idly rave, sir;
Though I am your wedded wife,
Yet I am not your slave, sir.
"One of two must still obey,
Nancy, Nancy;
Is it man or woman, say?
My spouse Nancy!"
"If it is still the lordly word,
Service and obedience;
I'll desert my sovereign lord—
And so, good by, allegiance!"
"Sad will I be, so bereft;
Nancy, Nancy!
Yet I'll try to make a shift,
My spouse Nancy!"
"My poor heart, then break it must,
My last hour I am near it;
When you lay me in the dust,
Think, think how you will bear it."

O, CAN YE SEW CUSHIONS?

O, can ye sew cushions and can ye sew sheets,
And can ye sing bal-lu-loo when the bairn greets?
And hee and baw birdie, and hee and baw lamb!
And hee and baw birdie, my bonnie wee lamb!
Hee, O, wee! O, what would I do wi' you;
Black is the life that I lead wi' you!
Money o' you—little for to gie you!
Hee, O, wee! O, what would I do wi' you?

WOMAN, COMPLAIN NOT!

Let not woman e'er complain
Of inconstancy in love;
Let not woman e'er complain
Fickle man is apt to rove.

Look abroad through Nature's range—
Nature's mighty law is change;
Ladies, would it not be strange,
Man should then a monster prove?

Mark the winds and mark the skies,
Ocean's ebb and ocean's flow;
Sun and moon but set to rise—
Round and round the seasons go.

Why, then, ask of silly man
To oppose great Nature's plan?
We'll be constant while we can—
You can be no more, you know.

JENNIE.

The following was written to Jean Jeffrey, daughter of a minister, who afterward became Mrs. Renwick, and emigrated to New York with her husband:

When first I saw fair Jennie's face
I couldna tell what ailed me;
My heart went fluttering pit-a-pat—
My een, they almost failed me.
She's aye sae neat, sae trim, sae tight
All grace does 'round her hover,
Ae look deprived me o' my heart
And I became a lover.

Had I Dundas' whole estate
Or Hopetown's wealth to shine in—
Did warlike laurels crown my brow
Or humbler bays entwining—
I'd lay them a' at Jennie's feet,
Could I but hope to move her

And prouder than a belted knight,
I'd be my Jennie's lover.
But sair I fear some happier swain
Has gained sweet Jennie's favor;
If so, may every bliss be hers,
Tho' I maun never have her.
But gang she east or gang she west,
'Twixt Forth and Tweed all over,
While men have eyes, or ears, or taste
She'll always find a lover.

The poet one day was taking a ride through the country on horseback and when he got to the town of Carlisle became thirsty and stopped at a tavern for a drink. He tethered his horse outside in the village green where it was espied by the poundmaster, who took it to the pound. When Burnsie came out he was mad clear through and this is what he wrote:

Was e'er puir poet sae befitted?
The maister drunk—the horse committed,
Puir harmless beast, tak thee nae care,
Thou'lt be a horse when he's nae mair (mare).

Andrew Turner was not highly appreciated by the poet, if we may judge from the following:

In seventeen hundred and forty-nine
Satan took stuff to make a swine
And cuist it in a corner;
But wilely he changed his plan
And shaped it something like a man
And called it Andrew Turner.

A MOTHERS ADDRESS TO HER INFANT.

My blessing upon thy sweet wee lippie,
My blessing upon thy bonnie e'e brie!
Thy smiles are sae like my blithe sodger laddie
Thou's aye the dearer and dearer to me.

NATIONAL THANKSGIVING ON A NAVAL VICTORY.

Ye hypocrites! are these your pranks,
To murder men and gi'e God thanks?
For shame gi'e o'er! proceed no further—
God won't accept your thanks for murther.

TO FOLLY.

The graybeard, Old Wisdom, may boast of his treasures—
Give me with gay Folly to live;
Grant him calm-blooded, time-settled pleasures

But Folly has raptures to give.

TO LORD GALLOWAY.

What dost thou in that mansion fair?
Flit, Galloway, and find
Some narrow, dirty dungeon cave,
The picture of thy mind!

No Stewart art thou, Galloway—
The Stewarts all were brave;
Besides, the Stewarts were but fools,
Not one of them a knave.

Bright ran thy line, O Galloway!
Through many a far-famed sire;
So ran the far-famed Roman way—
So ended—in a mire!

Spare me thy vengeance, Galloway—
In quiet let me live;
I ask no kindness at thy hand,
For thou hast none to give.

The poet subscribed for a paper which he didn't receive regularly, so he told the editor about it in this fashion:

Dear Peter, dear Peter,
We poor sons of meter
Are aften negleckit, ye ken;
For instance, your sheet, man,
Tho' glad I'm to see it, man,
I get no ae day in ten.

HONEST POVERTY.

Is there for honest poverty,
That hangs its head and a' that;
The coward slave, we pass him by,
We dare be poor for a' that;
For a' that and a' that!
Our toil's obscure and a' that,
The rank is but the guinea's stamp
The man's the gowd for a' that.

What though on hamely fare we dine
Wear hoddin grey and a' that;
Give fools their silks and knaves their wine
A man's a man for a' that!
For a' that and a' that,
Their tinsel show and a' that;

The honest man, though e'er sae poor,
Is king o' men for a' that!

Ye see yon birkie, ca'd a lord,
Wha' struts and stares and a' that?
Though hundreds worship at his word,
He's but a coof for a' that;
For a' that and a' that;
His riband, star and a' that,
The man of independent mind
He looks and laughs at a' that!

A prince can mak' a belted knight,
A marquis, duke and a' that;
But an honest man's aboon his might—
Guid faith he maunna fa' that;
For a' that and a' that,
Their dignities and a' that.
The pith o' sense, and pride o' worth,
Are higher ranks than a' that.

Then let us pray that come it may,
As come it will for a' that,
That sense and worth, o'er a' the earth
May bear the gree, and a' that!
For a' that and a' that
It's coming yet for a' that,
That man to man, the warld o'er,
Shall brothers be for a' that.

Here are a few facts concerning the personal and family history of the poet:

His father's name was William Burness, and was born November 11, 1721, at Clockenhill, Scotland. I suppose that Burness was the old-fashioned way of spelling Burns, hence the difference in the names of the son and father. The poet's name was Robert Burns and the father's William Burness, or Burns.

His mother's name was Agnes Brown and she was born in the Carrick district, Scotland, March 17, 1732.

Robert Burns, the great poet, was born January 25, 1759, and died July 21, 1796, being therefore not thirty-eight years of age at the time of his death. He was the eldest of seven children who were named consecutively Robert, Gilbert, Agnes, Arabella, William, John and Isabel.

The wife of the poet, as I have previously stated in this volume, was Jean Armour, and she was born at Mauchline in 1763 and died at Dumfries in 1834. She survived the poet many years and died at the ripe old age of 71. She was a national character and was made much of, as was everyone else intimately or even remotely connected with the National Bard. This is the reward of greatness, and thus any man or woman who achieves honorable greatness, leaves distinction behind them and throws a halo of glory over those with whom they have been connected or associated.

The following children were born to the great poet and his wife:

Twins in 1786. The boy, Robert, lived, but the girl died in infancy.

Twins in 1788. Both died in infancy.

Francis Wallace died at the age of 14.

William Nicol, born in 1791.

Elizabeth Riddell, born in 1792. Died at the age of two years.

James Glencairne, born in 1794, died in 1865.

Maxwell, born in 1796, died at the age of two.

It will be seen that the poet was the father of quite a number of children, some of whom lived to a ripe old age. Whether he was the father of any more children I am sure I don't know. If he was, almost any Scot will know it and can tell you more about it than I can. Bobbie was a very handsome man and was greatly admired by almost everyone, including the ladies. Some of his poems would lead one to believe that, like Byron,

> He was unskilled to cozen,
> And shared his love among a dozen.

but that may be mere poetic license. Poets, you know, have an eye for the *beautiful*, whether it be in landscape scenery, flowers, architecture, painting, statuary, the human form or what not. At any rate "Puir Rabbie" was the daddy of the children whose names I have given, for that is a matter of history. To show that the poet loved a joke himself, no matter on what subject, I here quote a little rhyme of his gotten off on a friend named James Smith who lived at Mauchline:

> Lament him, Mauchline husbands a'
> He aften did assist ye;
> For had ye stayed whole weeks awa'
> Your wives they n'er had missed ye.

In my short career I have run up against lots of folks who cannot take a joke or see the point of one and these poor people I pity, but do not blame, for they were born that way. I have always been poor but never proud and could take a joke—that is, when I could see the point of it. When I couldn't see the point of it I did not get angry.

Burnsie was a farmer and lived on ranches the most of his life. He was a hayseed from way back but as soon as he got celebrated high society began to run after him and the poor fellow couldn't keep away from it if he tried. It didn't take him long to learn how to make a bow without upsetting the table, but he was out of his element among the grand folks. Did he need polish to make him shine? I trow not. Wasn't his genius just as great before he struck society? Sure! But just to please folks he hobnobbed with them though he was as much out of his element as a fish when out of water. No doubt he wore a biled shirt and black claw-hammer coat and made his coat tails fly around pretty lively as he skipped around in a dance, but as society wanted him it got him. Had he lived long enough he might have been a baron, marquis, duke or count. Who can tell? While a plowman he scorned titles, but I wonder whether he would have rejected a patent of nobility had it been tendered him.

Genius is a complex quality. Samuel Smiles in his great work, "Self Help," says that genius is nothing more nor less than a capacity for taking infinite pains, and the world in general seems to have accepted his definition or explanation, but I, Windy Bill, an untutored savage from the Wild West, beg to differ wholly from Sam and I will "show you" why, and permit you to judge for yourself. Had Samuel defined *art* instead of genius as "an infinite capacity for taking pains" he might have been nearer the truth. Let us take the case of Burns. While plowing he wrote rhymes, but as he knew little or nothing of the art of versification he set his thoughts in mellifluous language of his own. Was it his thoughts or their setting that captivated people? His thoughts, of course, though the jingle made them more harmonious. Genius is the thought; art the setting. Tell me then that genius is a capacity for taking pains. Nary time. It comes forth spontaneous, natural, can't help itself. It is a God-given quality which lots of people possess to a greater or less degree. Musicians have it, as have painters, architects, writers, sculptors and people in all walks of life. Lots of poets in Scotland had genius long before our great friend Rabbie was born, and lots since them have had more or less of a share of the "divine afflatus," as some writers call it, but were any of them gifted as highly as Puir Rabbie? Not a one. Will another like him arise? Search me! There hasn't yet.

Notwithstanding that Rabbie was so highly gifted, he didn't know it. Don't you believe me? If you don't you needn't take my word for it, for I have evidence here that will prove it. I quote the preface that he wrote to the first book of his that ever was printed. Here it is:

> "The following trifles are not the production of the poet, who, with all the advantages of learned art and perhaps amid the elegancies and idleness of upper life looks down for a rural theme with an eye to Theocritus or Virgil. Unacquainted with the necessary requisites for commencing poetry by rule, he sings the sentiments and manners he felt and saw in himself and his rustic compeers around him, in his and their native language. Though a rhymer from his earlier years it was not till very lately that the applause (perhaps the partiality) of friendship awakened his vanity so as to make him think anything of his worth showing, for none of the poems were composed with a view to the press. To amuse himself with the little creations of his own fancy amid the toil and fatigue of a laborious life, these were his motives for courting the muses. Now that he appears in the public character of an author, he does it with fear and trembling. So dear is fame to the rhyming tribe that even he, an obscure, nameless bard, shrinks aghast at the thought of being branded as an impertinent blockhead, obtruding his nonsense on the world; and because he can make shift

to jingle a few doggerel Scottish rhymes together, looking upon himself as a poet of no small consequence, forsooth! If any critic catches at the word Genius, the author tells him, once for all, that he certainly looks upon himself as possessed of some poetic abilities, otherwise the publishing, in the manner he has done, would be a maneuver below the worst character his worst enemy will ever give him. But to the genius of an Allan Ramsay or a Robert Ferguson he has not the least pretension, nor ever had, even in his highest pulse of vanity. These two justly admired Scottish poets he has often had in his eye but rather to kindle in their flame than for servile imitation.

"To his subscribers the author returns his most sincere thanks—not the mercenary bow over a counter, but the heart-throbbing gratitude of the bard, conscious how much he owes to benevolence and friendship for gratifying him, if he deserves it, in that dearest wish of every poetic bosom—to be distinguished. He begs his readers, particularly the learned and the polite who may honor him with a perusal, that they will make every allowance for education and circumstances of life; but if, after a fair, candid and impartial criticism he shall stand convicted of dullness and nonsense let him be done by as he would in that case do by others—let him be condemned without mercy, to contempt and oblivion."

It is a queer fact that those mortals who possessed the greatest genius were always the most simple and diffident, and dubious about their own powers. They had a feeling in them that they were born to soar but they were hesitating, doubtful and did not know their very simplicity was a part of their greatness. They didn't appreciate their own capacities at first any more than are their capabilities appreciated by less gifted mortals. Before Burns' time Allan Ramsay and Robert Ferguson were looked upon as the greatest poets Scotland had ever produced, and so great were they that even Burns looked upon them with awe; and yet, unknown to himself, he was far greater than they. His generation may not have known it, but this generation does. Was Shakespeare appreciated in his generation? He was not. Was any truly great man? Hardly.

The earliest book of Burns that ever was put in print consisted of his minor poems which were written while he was in the fields plowing.

Of course he wasn't plowing always, so some were written while he was outdoors, here, there and everywhere in the vicinity of his country home. They were put into book-form by the advice of his friends and John Wilson at Kilmarnock, was the man who volunteered to do the printing. The book was a thin one, about half as thick as the ordinary novel of to-day, and it was agreed that only 612 books be struck off as a first edition. Mr. John Wilson was a long-headed printer and would not agree to print a single volume until at least 300 of the books had been subscribed for beforehand. He figured it out this way: "Suppose the book fails, where do I get off at? I set it up in type, do the binding, furnish the paper, pay the devil and the compositors, do the press work, make-up and all, so can I afford to take all the chances of getting any money out of this blooming poetry?" Mr. Wilson was a canny Scot and didn't propose to take any chances. He surely didn't lose anything in this venture, but whether he made anything I am unable to say.

Now, all of this is a very imperfect sketch of my old pard Burnsie, and if you care to know more about him I can refer you to quite a few biographies that have been written about him and are still being written about him by the score to this day. No less a personage than Sir Walter Scott has written a life history of him and so has the poet's own brother, Gilbert. Here is a list you can choose from:

Appeared

1.	Robert Heron (Life of Burns)	1797
2.	Dr. James Currie (Life and Works, 4 vols Works and Sketch of Life)	1800
3.	James Stover and John Grieg (Illustrated)	1804
4.	Robert Hartley Cromek (Reliques of Burns)	1808
5.	Lord Francis Jeffrey (Edinburgh Review)	1808
6.	Sir Walter Scott (Quarterly Review)	1808
7.	Dr. David Irving (Life of Burns)	1810
8.	Prof. Josiah Walker (Life and Poems, 2 vols)	1811
9.	Rev. Hamilton Paul (Life and Poems)	1819
10.	Gilbert Burns	1820
11.	Hugh Ainslie (Pilgrimage to the Land of Burns)	1822
13.	Alex. Peterkin (Life and Works, 4 vols)	1824
14.	John G. Lockhart (Life of Burns)	1828
15.	Thomas Carlyle (Edinburgh Review)	1828
16.	Allan Cunningham (Life and Works, 8 vols)	1834
17.	James Hogg and William Motherwell (Memoirs and Works, 5 vols.)	1854
18.	Prof. John Wilson (Essay on Genius)	1840
19.	W. C. McLehose (Correspondence)	1843
20.	Samuel Tyler (Burns as a Poet and Man)	1849
21.	Robert Chambers (Life and Works)	1851
22.	George Gilfillan (Memoirs and Works, 2 vols)	1856
23.	Rev. James White (Burns and Scott)	1858
24.	Rev. P. H. Waddell (Life and Works)	1859
25.	William Michael (Life and Works)	1871

CHAPTER XV.

SIR WALTER SCOTT.

Although Robert Burns is the idol of the Scotch people nowadays, it must not be supposed that he is the only one worshipped, for there is another man who is greatly revered, honored and loved. This man is Sir Walter Scott. The Scotch people affectionately call him Sir Walter and he did as much for his country as did Puir Rabbie. Both were Scotch to the backbone and loved their country as fondly and devotedly as any patriot can, but in their work they were totally dissimilar. Sir Walter started out as a writer of ballads, and chose for his themes historical subjects, mainly those connected with the ancient and modern history of his country. Burns, as I said before, remodeled and improved the old Scotch folk songs and in his democratic way described life around him in tuneful periods. Had he not been cut off in the flower of his prime he, too, might have been a great novelist for his great genius was capable of anything. He sprang from the masses and his heart was with the masses, but Sir Walter, who came from the classes had a heart for all, and described the lowly and humble as well as the great. Sir Walter's delineations of human character stand unrivalled today. He surely was proud of the fact that he was of gentle birth, which well he might have been, for that was no disgrace to him, any more than it is disgraceful to be of lowly birth, although in the old country blood counts for something. To show what Sir Walter thought of himself I here quote an extract from one of his works which he wrote himself:

> "My birth was neither distinguished nor sordid. According to the prejudices of my country, it was esteemed gentle, as I am connected, though remotely, with ancient families both by my father's and mother's side. My father's grandfather was Walter Scott, well known by the name of Beardie. He was the second son of Walter Scott, first lord of Raeburn, who was the third son of Sir Walter Scott and the grandson of Walter Scott, commonly called in tradition Auld Watt of Harden. I am therefore lineally descended from that chieftain, whose name I have made to ring in many a ditty, and from his fair dame, the Flower of Yarrow, no bad genealogy for a Border Minstrel."

Well, my poor friend Rabbie didn't spring from any border minstrel, but he was a born minstrel himself and could concoct a tune with the best of them. Mind you, I am not decrying Sir Walter, for that would be sacrilege, but Burnsie had nothing to brag of in the way of ancestry. Would Sir Walter have been less great had he sprung from common stock or would Robbie have been greater had he been blue-blooded? I am an American, an ex-member of Coxey's unwashed army, so I don't want to say yes or nay to this question. Let others decide.

Sir Walter's earliest success as a writer was won by discarding the conventionalities of art and creating a style of art his own. It takes a genius to do that. His style was simple, plain, and direct and won followers very quickly because it gained favor. This goes to show that if one has anything to say it is not necessary to say it in involved language, but just simply. Sir Walter's good common sense told him this was the fact and he acted accordingly. To say the honest truth some of Sir Walter's novels here and there are a little prolix, but there was a reason for it. Sir Walter was getting paid for space-writing. You don't believe me? I'll prove it. He went broke and to pay his debts—or rather those of the publishing house he unfortunately was connected with—he ground out "copy" as fast as he could, for every word of his was worth money. He begged his financial friends not to treat him like "a milch cow" but like a man, but as he was a money-maker they staid with him until all his money and property were gone and all he could earn until he died was swallowed up, too. His was another case like General Ulysses Simpson Grant.

Sir Walter was the ninth child in a very large family. His father was a methodical and industrious lawyer, and his mother a woman of much culture, refinement and imagination.

Of delicate health and lame from his second year, Sir Walter spent much of his childhood in the country with his relatives. At the fireside of neighbors he listened to the old ballads and stories of border warfare, which caused him at a very early age to acquire a taste for reading ancient history and to become imbued with a love for antiquarian research. When seven years of age he entered the High School of Edinburgh and attended it until twelve. When thirteen he entered the University of Edinburgh and decided on the profession of law. At the age of 21 he was admitted to the bar. He didn't like his profession, however, and spent much of his time in antiquarian research. When about 26 years of age he married Charlotte Margaret Carpenter, the daughter of a French Royalist, whose family after the death of the father had removed to England. Sir Walter and his wife lived first at Edinburgh and three years later rented a cottage at Lasswade. They remained at Lasswade six years and then took up their abode at Ashestiel. In 1799, when about 28 years of age, Sir Walter was made Deputy Sheriff of Selkirkshire to which was attached a salary of $1,500 per annum, and seven years afterward he was appointed a Clerk of Session with a salary of $3,500. He held down both jobs for 25 years, which proved he was a stayer. As his income was $5000 for 25 years it can be figured out about how much he earned. But Sir Walter wasn't a money-saver; he was a spender and a good provider. He kept open house and anyone who called received an old-fashioned Scotch welcome, and I know from my sojourn in Scotland what that means. It means you're welcome to stay or welcome to go, but while you do stay the best is none too good for you. Sir Walter's hospitality was of that sort and while holding down both jobs he was doing a little literary work on the side. First came ballads, then poems of romance and later novels. He was getting along first rate financially so he concluded to take up his residence at Abbottsford, a palatial mansion. By this time he had already gained fame and much lucre and was run after by the "hoi-polloi," the "would-be could-be's" and the Great. The doors of Abbottsford opened wide for all. Even the poor were given "a hand-out" of some kind. Too bad Billy and me wasn't alive then. But this was before our time, about a hundred years or so. Oh what a place for grafters Abbottsford must have been! Sir Walter was easy. So easy was he, in fact, that the publishing house of Ballantyne & Co., which roped him in as a side partner, went flewy and left Sir Walter to foot all the bills. Sir Walter was an honorable man and prized honor above wealth, so he turned over everything he had, including Abbottsford, to the alleged creditors, but there was not enough to satisfy claims. The debt amounted to several hundred thousand dollars. Thereupon he continued writing novels and wrote as he never wrote before. He ground out ten novels in six years and had paid up about $200,000, when his health began to fail. The pace was too swift for a man sixty years of age, which he was then. The creditors were insatiable and were greedy for the last farthing. Business is business, said they.

When a little over sixty years of age Sir Walter had a stroke of paralysis caused by overwork and worry, and was recommended by his physicians to take a sea voyage. He embarked for Italy in a frigate which was placed at his disposal by the English government, but sad to relate, the trip benefited him but little. He visited Rome, Venice and other places, but came home a few months afterward to die. "Man's inhumanity to man" killed Sir Walter before his time.

Sir Walter's manner was that of a gentleman and he was amiable, unaffected and polished. He was simple and kindly and approachable by all. Much of his literary work was done at Ashestiel, but more at Abbottsford. He kept open house everywhere. He arose at five o'clock in the morning and wrote until eight o'clock. He then breakfasted with his family and after putting in an hour or so with them returned to his writings. He worked until noon and then was his own man, to do as he liked. During the afternoon he put in some time with his guests, gave reporters interviews, was snap-shotted by cameras, saw that the dogs got enough to eat, gave orders to the servants that if too many 'bos came around to sick the dogs on them and then he went a horseback or a carriage riding. In the evening there was some social chat, after which Sir Walter retired early. That was the routine.

This master in the art of novel writing was fully six feet in height, well proportioned and well built with the exception of a slight deformity in the ankle, which I have alluded to before. His face was of a Scotch cast, heavy and full; the forehead was high and broad, the head lofty, the nose short, the upper lip long, and the expression of his features kindly. I have seen dead loads of pictures, images and statues of Sir Walter, yet hardly two of them were alike. I consider Sir Walter a handsome man and to me there seems to be something grand and noble in the cast of his countenance. I *know* the light of genius was there, and maybe that is why he so impresses me, but with it all his features have a noble cast. He is goodly to look upon, surely.

To tell the truth, I don't read much poetry, but some competent critic who has read Sir Walter's has this to say of it:

> "The distinctive features of the poetry of Scott are ease, ra-

pidity of movement, a spirited flow of narrative that holds our attention, an out-of-door atmosphere and power of natural description, an occasional intrusion of a gentle personal sadness and but little more. The subtle and mystic element so characteristic of the poetry of Wordsworth and Coleridge is not to be found in that of Scott, while in lyrical power he does not approach Shelley. We find instead an intense sense of reality in all his natural descriptions; it surrounds them with an indefinable atmosphere, because they are so transparently true. Scott's first impulse in the direction of poetry was given to him from the study of the German ballads, especially Burger's Lenore, of which he made a translation. As his ideas widened, he wished to do for Scottish Border life what Goethe had done for the ancient feudalism of the Rhine. He was at first undecided whether to choose prose or verse as the medium; but a legend was sent him by the Countess of Dalkeith with a request that he would put it in ballad form. Having thus the framework for his purpose, he went to work, and "The Lay of the Last Minstrel" was the result. The battle scene in Marmion has been called the most Homeric passage in modern literature, and his description of the Battle of Beal au Duine from "The Lady of the Lake" is an exquisite piece of narration from the gleam of the spears in the thicket to the death of Roderick Dhu at its close. In the deepest sense Scott is one with the spirit of his time in his grasp of fact, in that steadily looking at the object which Wordsworth had fought for in poetry, which Carlyle had advocated in philosophy. He is allied, too, to that broad sympathy for man which lay closest to the heart of the age's literary expression. Wordsworth's part is to inspire an interest in the lives of men and women about us; Scott's to enlarge the bounds of our sympathy beyond the present, and to people the silent centuries. Shelley's inspiration is hope for the future; Scott's is reverence for the past."

I have read a few of Sir Walter's novels, and some of them several times, and every time I read them it is with renewed interest. His delineation of human character is so true to nature and so graphic that I feel the living, speaking person before me as I read. If that ain't writing I would like to know what is. Whether it be peasant, servant, knight, esquire, king, lord, lady or girl, all are shown up on the screen so plainly that I take it all as a matter of course and say nothing. It is all so plain and simple that there is nothing to say. That is art and the highest form of it. It is next to nature.

Art and genius are closely allied. It is not everyone who loves the "altogether" or the "realistic," which may be well. Were it not so, many poets, painters, sculptors, musicians and other handicraftsmen would be left out in the cold, with none to do him reverence. All tastes happily are catered to, so everyone is happy.

As I am neither a critic nor a biographer I shall endeavor to give my readers an idea what Sir Walter was thought of by others and will quote the language they used.

George Tichnor, the author, says that Scott repeated to him the English translations of two long Spanish ballads which he had never seen, but which had been read to him twice.

Scott's college friend, John Irving, in writing of himself and Scott, says: "The number of books we thus devoured was very great. I forgot a great part of what I read; but my friend, notwithstanding he read with such rapidity, remained, to my surprise, master of it all, and could even, weeks and months afterwards, repeat a whole page in which anything had particularly struck him at the moment."

Washington Irving remarked: "During the time of my visit he inclined to the comic rather than to the grave in his anecdotes and stories; and such, I was told, was his general inclination. He relished a joke or a trait of humor in social intercourse, and laughed with right good will.... His humor in conversation, as in his works, was genial and free from causticity. He had a quick perception of faults and foibles, but he looked upon human nature with an indulgent eye, relishing what was good and pleasant, tolerating what was frail and pitying what was evil.... I do not recollect a sneer throughout his conversation, any more than there is throughout his works."

Lord Byron said: "I think that Scott is the only very successful genius that could be cited as being as generally beloved as a man as he is admired as an author; and I must add, he deserves it, for he is so thoroughly good-natured, sincere and honest, that he disarms the envy and jealousy his extraordinary genius must excite."

Leslie Stephen remarked: "Scott could never see an old tower, or a bank, or a rush of a stream without instantly recalling a boundless collection of appropriate anecdotes. He might be quoted as a case in point by those who would explain all poetical imagination by the power of associating ideas. He is the *poet of association*."

Lockhart, who married the daughter of Sir Walter and who was therefore his son-in-law, wrote a biography of his father-in-law wherein he says that: "The love of his country became indeed a passion; no knight ever tilted for his mistress more willingly than he would have bled and died to preserve even the airiest surviving nothing of her antique pretensions for Scotland. But the Scotland of his affections had the clan *Scott* for her kernel."

I believe the son-in-law is inclined to be facetious, but is he *just* to his immortal father-in-law? I don't believe he is—therefore his criticisms are not worth a whoop.

Thomas Carlyle, the cynical philosopher and mugwump, condescended to give Sir Walter a sort of recommendation of character, which it renders me extremely happy to quote. Here it is. Read it carefully and ponder:

"The surliest critic must allow that Scott was a genuine man, which itself is a great matter. No affectation, fantasticality or distortion dwelt in him; no shadow of cant. Nay, withal, was he not a right brave and strong man according to his kind? What a load of toil, what a measure of felicity he quietly bore along with him! With what quiet strength he both worked on this earth and enjoyed in it, invincible to evil fortune and to good!"

This cynic, this philosopher, this mugwump says Sir Walter was a *genuine man.* Good for Mr. Carlyle.

Everyone was proud to call Sir Walter "friend," and he was just great enough to be happy to call those who were worthy, his friend. Among his great friends were the following:

John Irving, who was an intimate college friend. I have quoted him in regard to the number of books read by Sir Walter.

Robert Burns came to Edinburgh when Sir Walter was fifteen years of age, and Sir Walter's boyish admiration for the National Bard was great. In after life, when Sir Walter became great, he wrote a great deal concerning Puir Rabbie. And it is worth reading.

James Ballantyne, Sir Walter's partner in the publishing business, was a good friend.

So was James Hogg, the poet peasant, sometimes called "The Ettrick Shepherd."

And so was Thomas Campbell, the poet, author of "The Pleasures of Hope."

The poet William Wordsworth was a lifelong friend.

Robert Southey, the poet, visited Sir Walter at Ashestiel and was admired by him greatly.

Joanna Baillie, the poetess, was a warm friend.

So was Lord Byron.

Sir Humphry Davy, the philosopher, visited Sir Walter and was well liked by him.

Goethe, the German poet, was a warm admirer and friend of Sir Walter.

So was Henry Hallam, the historian; Crabbe, the poet; Maria Edgeworth, the novelist; George Ticknor, the author; Dugald Stewart, Archibald Alison, Sydney Smith, Lord Brougham, Lord Jeffrey, Thomas Erskine, William Clerk, Sir William Hamilton, etc., etc.

Last but not least among those who regarded Sir Walter as a friend and who were so regarded by him was our own countryman, Washington Irving. Our own "Washy" was an author, too, and one not to be sneezed at. Sir Walter regarded him highly and Washy dropped in on him, casual like, at Abbottsford. Washy had written some good things himself, but had found it difficult to win recognition. Sir Walter stood sponsor for him and told the world it ought to be ashamed of itself not to recognize merit of so high an order. Thereupon the world promptly did recognize our Washy. Did our Washy need a sponsor? Well, hardly. No American ever lived who was an abler or more polished writer than he. Will you please show me a man who can beat our Washy. You can't do it. Smile at me if you will, but I doubt if even Sir Walter himself was so much superior to him. Have you read Irving's Astoria, a true and lifelike history of the Northwest? or his Rip Van Winkle, or his sketches, the Alhambra, etc.? Irving's is another case where a great man failed of appreciation at first.

Well, my countrymen, our Washy is dead, but we appreciate him now just the same. The United States never produced a writer more polished and able than he, and it is rather humiliating to think that a great foreigner had to apprise us of his merits.

To wind up this chapter on Sir Walter Scott I will give you a list of his writings, arranged in chronological order:

BALLADS.

Glenfinlas, 1799.
Eve of St. John, 1799.
The Grey Brothers, 1799.
Border Minstrelsy, 1802-1803.
Cadyow Castle, 1810.
English Minstrelsy, 1810.
The Battle of Sempach, 1818.
The Noble Moringer, 1819.
The Lay of the Last Minstrel, 1805.
Marmion, 1808.
The Lady of the Lake, 1810.
Vision of Don Roderick, 1811.
Rokeby, 1812.
The Bridal of Triermain, 1813.
The Lord of the Isles, 1815.

PROSE WORKS.

Waverley, 1814.
Guy Mannering, 1815.
The Antiquary, 1816.
The Black Dwarf, 1816.
Old Mortality, 1816.
Rob Roy, 1818.
The Heart of Mid-Lothian, 1818.
The Bride of Lammermoor, 1819.
The Legend of Montrose, 1819.
Ivanhoe, 1820.
The Monastery, 1820.
The Abbott, 1820.
Kenilworth, 1821.
The Pirate, 1822.
The Fortunes of Nigel, 1822.
Peveril of the Peak, 1823.
Quentin Durward, 1823.
St. Ronan's Well, 1824.

Red Gauntlet, 1824.
The Betrothed, 1825.
The Talisman, 1825.
Woodstock, 1826.
The Two Drovers, 1827.
The Highland Widow, 1827.
The Surgeon's Daughter, 1827.
The Fair Maid of Perth, 1828.
Anne of Geierstein, 1829.
Count Robert of Paris, 1831.
Castle Dangerous, 1831.

Lector House believes that a society develops through a two-fold approach of continuous learning and adaptation, which is derived from the study of classic literary works spread across the historic timeline of literature records. Therefore, we aim at reviving, repairing and redeveloping all those inaccessible or damaged but historically as well as culturally important literature across subjects so that the future generations may have an opportunity to study and learn from past works to embark upon a journey of creating a better future.

This book is a result of an effort made by Lector House towards making a contribution to the preservation and repair of original ancient works which might hold historical significance to the approach of continuous learning across subjects.

HAPPY READING & LEARNING!

LECTOR HOUSE LLP
E-MAIL: lectorpublishing@gmail.com